IMAGES OF ENGLAND

BRIGHTON
COLLEGE

Toya M. Heath

30th June, 2007

S. MATTHEWS CH.

COLLEGE TERRACE

WALPOLE ROAD

FIVES COURTS

SUTHERLAND ROAD

PAVILION

PLAYING FIELDS

CLASS ROOMS

KEMP TOWN STATION

PHYSICAL LAB & WORKSHOPS

TUCK SHOP

FIVES COURTS

DINING HALL

HEAD MASTERS HOUSE

SWIMMING BATH

CHAPEL

WAR MEMORIAL

SCHOOL HALL ARMOURY UNDER

CHICHESTER HOUSE

BUILDINGS CORRESPONDING TO THOSE ON THE OTHER SIDE OF ENTRANCE TO BE ERECTED HERE

BRISTOL HOUSE

EASTERN ROAD

G. G. WOODWARD

COLLEGE ROAD

ΤΟ ΔΕΥ ΝΙΚΑΤΟ

IMAGES OF ENGLAND

BRIGHTON COLLEGE

JOYCE HEATER

TEMPUS

Frontispiece: This drawing was published in 1925 and shows how
the College was surrounded by the expansion of the town towards
the east. To the west is the branch line from Brighton to Kemp
Town Station, long-since closed. The houses on the other side of
Sutherland Road have not yet been built and St Matthew's church
still stands at the north-west corner of the playing fields. It has been
replaced by a block of flats, St Matthew's Court.

First published 2007

Tempus Publishing Limited
The Mill, Brimscombe Port,
Stroud, Gloucestershire, GL5 2QG
www.tempus-publishing.com

British Library Cataloguing in Publication Data.
A catalogue record for this book is available from the British Library.

ISBN 978 0 7524 4300 3

Typesetting and origination by Tempus Publishing Limited.
Printed in Great Britain.

Contents

Acknowledgements

Philip Burstow wrote the first clear narrative of College history which was published in 1957. In 1995, to mark the 150th anniversary of the founding of the School, Martin Jones produced his scholarly and definitive volume. To both of them, two of my predecessors in the Archives, I here acknowledge my debt and gratitude.

A number of members of the Common Room have been helpful in identifying former pupils and answering factual queries. Thank you to Keren Burton, Sandy Chenery, Michael Curameng-Henderson, Elizabeth Cody, Ken Grocott, Damon Kerr, Philip Robinson, Edward Twohig and Tony Whitestone.

Thank you also to Simon Smith and Jo-anne Riley for encouragement and support.

David Lowe has helped with some of the photographs and I am grateful for his expertise.

My main acknowledgement has to be to Fiona Aiken. She has encouraged and supported me when the obstacles were daunting, has shown endless patience with my ignorance of computers, has deciphered my manuscript and produced an immaculate typescript. Without her help the project would not have been possible.

All royalties will help to provide bursaries for talented pupils who would not otherwise be able to attend Brighton College.

Introduction

The history of the College has already been written and it is far too soon to produce a reassessment of Martin Jones' thesis. This book is not intended in any way to change or replace it. It takes a different approach based on photographic evidence. It is obvious that there are some aspects of the College's past which have no visual image, and therefore the compilation of a series of pictures does not produce the whole story.

This book is also part of a series and has to adhere to the structure set out by the publisher. The number of pages is limited and the reader may be frustrated by the absence of a particular person or event. From its nature this volume cannot be comprehensive.

The main topic which cannot appear in picture form is the academic standing of the School. There are a few references but I set out here a brief outline. The members of the teaching staff in 1847 were unusually highly qualified and the new School quickly gained a formidable reputation for scholarship. Intellectual attainment was cherished. The subjects taught were the Classics (a tradition which lasted for many years), reading, writing and arithmetic. Lessons in drawing, singing, Italian, Hebrew and Urdu were extra. In 1852 science lessons, unusual at the time, were introduced by the Second Principal. Also in those days of Empire he added Hindustani, Sanskrit and Persian. There is a link here with the recent introduction of Mandarin to the current curriculum. From the beginning boys went on to Oxford and Cambridge and three 'firsts' were achieved in 1851. By the 1880s all forms studied mathematics, divinity, English literature, French, Latin and history. The classics were still important but German, geometrical drawing and advanced science became part of the timetable for those who chose the 'modern' side. These boys were aiming for the Army or Navy or the Civil Service. The classical side prepared pupils for the universities and the professions (the Church and the Law). Academic distinctions gained by Old Brightonians were impressive for a small school. In the early years of the twentieth century the standard of work and teaching remained high.

The problem came after 1918 as a direct result of Canon Dawson's need to raise numbers and thus increase income. His policy was to accept anyone regardless of ability and he appointed staff for their rugby or cricket skills rather than academic qualification. The inspectors in 1930 gave a less than favourable report. Standards recovered especially after the appointment of some very highly qualified men and were maintained during the war. They continued to rise and seven open awards and ten state scholarships were won in 1955-56.

By this time one third of the School were in the Sixth Form. The curriculum expanded and sixty-one per cent of boys leaving with A-levels went to university by 1968. Academically the College has never looked back and the most recent Oxbridge offers which appear at the end of the book are a source of pride. These results have been achieved by young men and women who also participate fully in the broader life of the School. The talented musician or the outstanding rugby player, because of their commitment, are likely to excel academically as well.

The story of the College which follows is one of resilience. It has faced bankruptcy and the threat of closure more than once. It has adapted to social and educational change in order to survive. It has not, however, sacrificed ideals in the process and remains true to the vision of its founder.

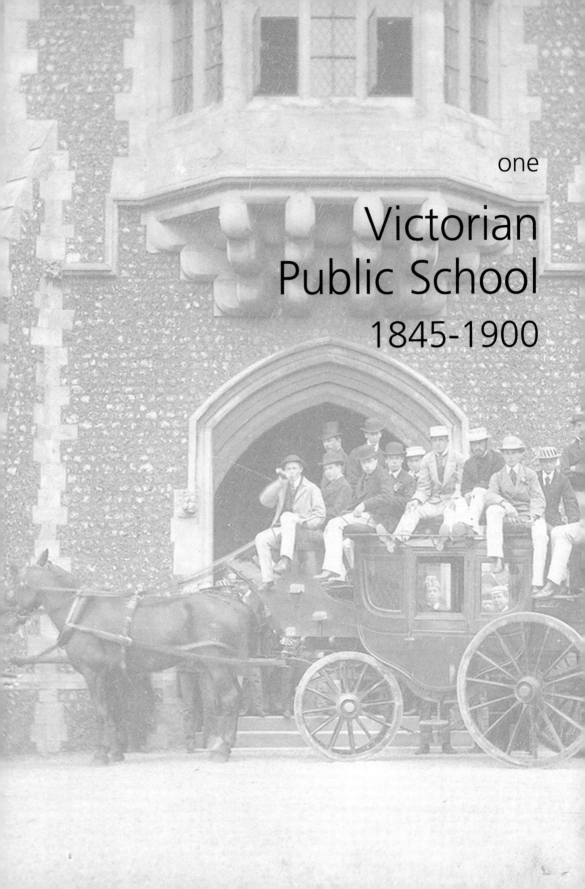

one

Victorian
Public School

1845-1900

Beginnings

The royal patronage enjoyed by Brighton since the Prince of Wales had made his first visit in 1783, and which had continued during the reign of William IV and Adelaide, was quickly withdrawn by Queen Victoria. As early in her reign as 1842 she wrote of the town, 'the people here are very indiscreet and troublesome which makes this place quite a prison'. The young royal family sought privacy at Osborne and Prinny's Pavilion was to be sold at the very time that Brighton College was being planned. Fortunately for the town the College Council could not afford to buy the royal residence for their school and Brighton's most well-known landmark remained for posterity. It was not surprising that a request, 'that Her Majesty will graciously consider to become the Patron of the Proposed College' was politely declined. Most appropriately the second choice for the first patron of the new Church of England foundation was the Bishop of Chichester.

The National School, Church Street (c. 1830) where the idea for a proprietary College at Brighton was first discussed in July 1845 at a private meeting of prominent local worthies. The Chairman was the Vicar of Brighton, the Revd Henry Wagner. At a later public meeting it was resolved to establish the College, 'on Church of England principles for the education of the sons of noblemen and gentlemen'. The earliest College buildings are still in constant use. The National School was less fortunate. A superb and rare example of Regency Gothic architecture, it was tragically demolished in 1971 when a postal strike delayed the delivery to Brighton Council of a Grade II listing document.

William Aldwin Soames with his family, *c.* 1870. His memorial tablet in the Chapel states that he, 'conceived the idea of Brighton College and in the year 1845 took the principal part in founding it'. Himself a man of vision, he was also able to inspire others and it was he who gathered the original committee together. In the roles of treasurer, joint honorary secretary and trustee he strove tirelessly for his creation. He bought the first four shares, personally underwrote the £6,000 mortgage in 1859 when funds were low and continued to serve on the College Council until shortly before his death in 1871. Martin Jones has described him as 'our forgotten founder'. We hope that this situation will be remedied by the recent establishment of the Soames Society (2006), the idea of David Gold, current President of the Old Brightonians' Association and College Development Director.

Left to right, front row: Mrs Soames, W.A. Soames, Florence Soames. Back row: Louisa Soames, W.A. Soames, junior, Laura Soames, Arthur Soames, Henry Soames and his wife, Constance.

All his sons attended the College.

The Revd Arthur Macleane was appointed as the first Principal in the summer of 1846. He had been educated at Winchester and Trinity College, Cambridge, was married and about to be ordained priest. He was a scholar of distinction, having gained a double first in maths and classics and, in an age far removed from our own, no one questioned this choice of a candidate who had never set foot in a classroom since he had left school! He had, however, had practical experience in India and his theological opinions were regarded as impeccable – he was an evangelical and the Anglican churchmanship of the Council was firmly of the same persuasion. The ethos of the new School would be in safe hands.

In May 1846 the Council decided to take out a three-year lease on Lion House, Portland Place. Teaching began there in January 1847 with forty-seven boys on the Roll. Meanwhile a search was under way for land on which to build the College and the present site, then named Bakers Bottom, was finally chosen. Early in the twentieth century the Lion House was acquired by St Dunstan's for the care of soldiers blinded in the First World War and was later renamed Pearson House.

George Gilbert Scott (later knighted) was the winner of the architectural competition organised by the College Council in January 1848. The candidates were asked to design a day and boarding school for 600 boys aged from nine to twenty years. Gilbert Scott became the most prolific of High Victorian architects and his designs included the Albert Memorial, the Foreign Office, Glasgow University and St Mary's Cathedral in Edinburgh. The Council was able to raise about half of the advertised sum for the scheme and thus only the central building of classrooms and studies for senior Masters was completed by 1849. This is now called the Main Building.

George Gilbert Scott's winning design for Brighton College. The cloister planned for the south front is clearly shown but was never built. This economy saved £664.

Above: Laying the foundation stone, 27 June 1848. The stone has no inscription, but underneath is an engraved brass plate:

> The 1st stone of this College was laid
> On the 27th day of June
> AD MDCCCXLVIII
> By the Right Reverend Father in God
> Ashurst Turner Gilbert, D.D.
> Lord Bishop of Chichester

The stone is inside the south-west wall of the porch to the Main Building and is not visible. Below it were placed some coins, College papers and a copy of *The Times* for that day.

Opposite: Three sections of a cartoon drawn by Alfred Thompson, a pupil aged seventeen. The whole drawing shows the procession from the Lion House, Portland Place to the foundation ceremony at Bakers Bottom. Top: The Council in the carriage followed by the Treasurer (W.A. Soames) on horseback. Middle: Peelers (policemen of their day) escorting the mounted Principal who carries a pile of prizes, followed by a group of *praepositors* (the equivalent of prefects). Bottom: The Lower School, a large number of small, top-hatted figures watched by *spectators*.

From the very beginning the College has used the Greek motto shown on this device. This choice of language was unique among English schools; the rest used Latin or English. The motto is a quotation from *Agamemnon*, a play by Aeschylus (*c.* 458 BC). The translation of the lines from which it is taken is *Sing the song of sorrow, sorrow,* **yet let good prevail**.

Brighton College, *c.* 1865. This print dates from the end of the first phase of building. On the right stands the Principal's house, designed by Gilbert Scott and built 1852-53. It provided accommodation on site for boarders as well as a home for the Principal's family. To the south-west of the Main Building is the Chapel built in 1859, also to Scott's design. The new boundary walls created a screen from the road to the south, and a further improvement came with the connecting of the College to the town gas main in 1855-56.

The interior of the College Chapel as it was built in 1859. The Council, anxious to restrict the cost, ordered the cheapest country church pattern from Scott. After he had submitted his design for a short single-cell building they asked him to make all possible reductions. There was therefore a minimum of carving and neither stained glass nor coloured marble. Nor was that all. Funding was raised retrospectively by charging a compulsory annual fee for 'seating in the Chapel'. This photograph is of a painting by Alfred Gray in 1864. He was a pupil at the time. In 1923, when Rector of Filby in Norfolk, he presented his picture to the College.

Very early in its history the College established itself as a place of sporting excellence. This was a remarkable achievement for a small school where games were recreational and completely voluntary. They did not become compulsory until 1902. In 1852 the *Brighton College Magazine* stated that 'Cricket will always retain its place as the head of all games in this country' and in that same year Herbert Southey White was the first Old Brightonian to win a cricket blue.

The First XI, 1865. This was possibly the earliest of the College's unbeaten sides. The photograph was presented by Stephen Barker, son of George Gompertz Barker who stands fifth from the left with arms folded. Only two other players are definitely identified. They are numbers seven and eight from the left, G.C. Barnes and H. Dealtry.

Opposite above: The Playground (now the Home Ground) before enlargement, 1876. The rough state of the Playground caused problems in the early days. Tonbridge complained about the wicket in 1858 and a sheep drover's right of way across the pitch did not improve matters. The photographer was looking north-east across Bakers Bottom to Whitehawk Hill. The houses on the left are Canning Street (built 1859-64). As yet neither College Terrace nor Walpole Terrace had appeared. In 1883 the Playground was finally levelled and reached the size and shape we know today.

Opposite below: Off to the match. The XI ready to leave for Lancing, 1871. Lancing won by two runs.

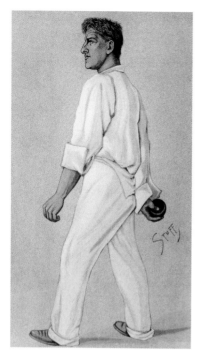

Left: 'Sammy' Woods (1884-1886). In the 1880s the College produced a group of superb, all-round sportsmen and of these S.M.J. Woods was the most outstanding. He was one of the undefeated XI of 1885, played for Sussex while still at School, Captained Cambridge and Somerset and played for Australia v England in 1888. He also played Association Football for Australia, rugby three times for Cambridge v Oxford and won thirteen England caps. In his first-class career he made nineteen centuries and 15,499 runs and took 1,079 wickets.

Below: The unbeaten First XI, 1885. Left to right, back row: C.H. Bond, W.S. Paskin, F.H. O'Donoghue, S.M.J. Woods, H.C. Cooper, W. Harris. Front row: H.D.L. Woods, G.H. Cotterill (Captain), G.R. Wilson, L.C. Raymond. Seated on ground: W.J. Richardson

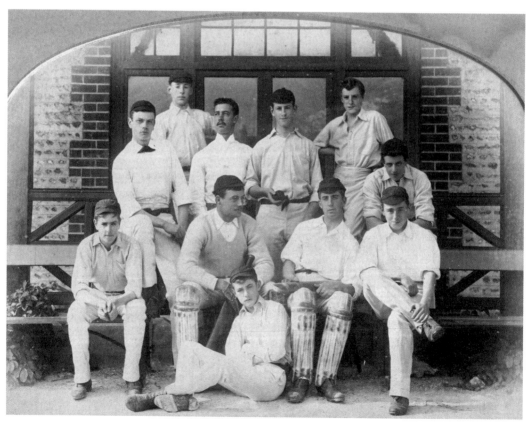

Football was the major winter sport until it was replaced by rugby in 1918. As in cricket the College produced some very fine players in the 1880s. Four won their blues and played for England. When football took over the Lent term in 1885 there was a rapid decline in the game of fives which had been played since 1851. From 1847 the boys swam in the sea and at Brill's Baths and in 1856 an athletics sports' meeting was staged for the first time. 'Paper chases' or 'hare and hounds' (a form of cross-country running) were abolished around 1900, possibly because some pupils seem to have suffered ill-effects from courses as long as thirteen miles! Gymnastics was part of the curriculum and boxing and fencing were also taught.

Below: Football First XI, 1888–89. Winners of the Senior Sussex Cup. From left to right, back row: A.L. King, F. Harvey, L.H. Gay, A.T. Hay, Esq., R. Young, F.E. Parsons. Front row: G.M. Robinson, G.W. Picton, N.C. Cooper (Captain), H.C. Holland, F.E. Whiteley, A.G. Cavendish.

Above: A group in the fives court, *c.*1880. Fives was the most significant game played in the Lent term even though it occupied only a small number of pupils. Its rapid decline followed the football takeover in 1885. School games were becoming more serious and the team spirit, encouraged by football and cricket, was regarded as of greater importance than individual success. After a revival in the twentieth century the courts were finally demolished in 1966. The Pre-Prep School now stands on the site.

Left: Sergeant Reynolds, the Gymnastic Instructor, *c.* 1896. The Lecture Hall, built in 1859, was later set up as the first gymnasium in an English school. An Old Boy, Sir George Fox, was Inspector of Army Gymnasia, 1897-1910. The room became the Chapel Music Room and finally it was completely refurbished in 1995. The opening ceremony was performed by Sir Michael Hordern after whom it is named. His early interest in drama began while he was a pupil here.

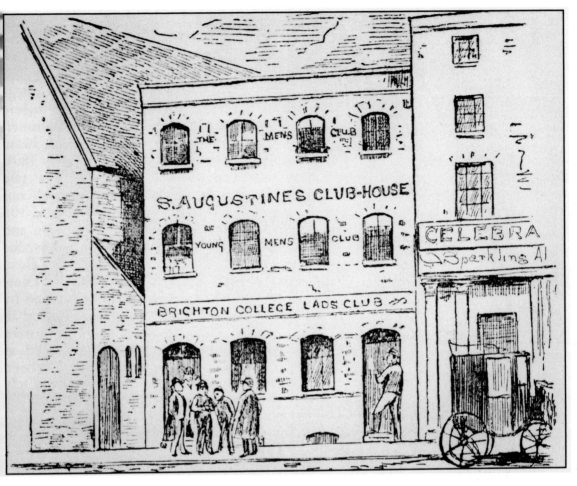

The Brighton College Mission, Stepney, c. 1890. Public schools and universities set up Missions in poor urban areas in the second half of the nineteenth century. There was a desire to spread the Christian faith but also to alleviate the widespread poverty in our cities. Britain ruled the world's largest empire and yet thousands of its own people faced permanent destitution. In 1885 the Headmaster, the Revd Thomas Hayes Belcher, set up a scheme for a College Mission which was based in the slum parish of St Augustine in Stepney. The vicar and curate were brothers, Harry and Richard Wilson, and both were Old Brightonians. Money was raised in the College to support a club which was run by the church for local boys. It offered some basic facilities such as cheap food and football and cricket but only to those who would attend church. Some of the boys visited Brighton and OBs were asked to help out at the club. The premises were completely renovated and the vicar reported an increase in the number of communicants at Easter 1894. It would seem that both aims of the Mission were to some extent being fulfilled. However, all references in Brighton College records stop in 1899 and no evidence has been found to explain the apparent breaking of the connection. It was not until the early 1920s that a new home Mission was launched to the Brighton slum parish of St John, Carlton Hill. The church of St Augustine, Stepney was gutted in the Blitz and later demolished. The clubhouse still stands.

From 1847 the College had an 'Organist and Choral Master', but music was not part of the curriculum and until 1888 the Master was part-time and his name appeared with those of the drawing and fencing Masters at the end of the list of staff. The first to hold the position was Thomas Ingram and he was expected to give singing lessons, train the Chapel Choir and play for services. He was portrayed in the cartoon of 1848. His successor, Robert Taylor, also appears in cartoon form on the next page. In 1888 the first full- time Music Master was appointed, George Sampson, and he is shown in the photograph of the Choir. The programme which follows is of the annual Christmas concert in 1888. No orchestra features though one had been formed by 1891. The last item was the first public performance of the School Song. The words had been written by William Douglas Eggar, an Old Brightonian who was also on the College staff.

Opposite above: Another section from the cartoon of 1848. G.P. Burstow, in his *History of Brighton College*, describes the figures as they appear:

Ingram with his cravat and large pin is portrayed first, and in the Choir besides White, the leader, and T. G. Clarke, the leading treble, can be seen a figure with a small tuning fork. He is E. R. Hudleston, a boy who was constantly criticising his fellows and saying they were out of tune. A barrel organ appears – a sly dig here, for an organ did not exist at the College for many years to come.

Opposite below: The Choir, 1892. From left to right, back row: Fort, Smith, Belcher, A.L. Bowley, Esq, Hills, Bird, A.B. Belcher, Esq, Smith, Belcher, Barnes, Playne, C.J. Mayne, Esq. Middle row: Saunders, Cobb, Crampton, Holmes, G. Sampson, Esq, Kagar, Hills, Rutter, Holmes, Barnes. Front row: Gillespie, Tadman, Cobb, Harris, Harris, Rutter, Neame, Etlinger, Wix.

Robert Taylor, Choir Master and Organist (1870-88). In 1871 the *Brighton Gazette* reported a College Concert which included a selection from Handel's *Joshua*. In 1885 there was a Choir Picnic (the only one ever mentioned). About fifty boys and Masters left Kemp Town Station for Bramber. The luncheon was taken near the river Adur and the food was delivered by a provision-boat.

PROGRAMME.

PART I.

Part Song ...	"O who will o'er the downs so free" ...		*Pearsall.*
	THE CHOIR.		
Violin Solo	"Le Rêve"		*Goldermann.*
	E. SELOUS.		
Song	"Tom Bowling"		*Dibdin.*
	THE REV. T. HAYES BELCHER.		
Organ Solo	Sonata No. 9		*Corelli.*
	(Largo—Gigue—Gavotte.)		
	MR. GEORGE SAMPSON.		
Duet	"Greeting" ...		*... Mendelssohn.*
	THE TREBLES.		
Pianoforte Solo	Invitation (with Arabesques)		*Weber-Tausig,*
	MRS. GRAMSHAW.		
Song	.. "Tell her I love her so"		*De Faye.*
	W. DE V. LE MAISTRE.		
Song	"Ave Maria"		*Smart.*
	THE CHOIR.		

PART II.

Part Song ...	"O, hush thee, my Babie" ...		*Sullivan.*
	THE CHOIR.		
Violin Solo ...	Andante from Violin Concerto		*... Mendelssohn.*
	E. SELOUS.		
Song	"She wore a Wreath of Roses" ...		*... Loder.*
	THE REV. T. HAYES BELCHER.		
Organ Solo ...	{ *a.* The Funeral March of a Marionette		*Gounod.*
	{ *b.* Andante in G		*Batiste.*
	MR. GEORGE SAMPSON.		
Duet	... "Autumn"		*... Mendelssohn.*
	THE TREBLES.		
Song	... "On the Rolling Wave" ...		*Godfrey Marks.*
	MR. C. H. BOND.		
Pianoforte Solo ...	"Mazurka"		*... B. Godard.*
	MRS. GRAMSHAW.		
"THE BRIGHTON COLLEGE SONG"			*SAMPSON.*
	THE CHOIR AND SCHOOL.		

"GOD SAVE THE QUEEN."

Opposite: College Concert, December 1888. The review in the *Brighton College Magazine* reports:

Then came the gem of the evening in the Headmaster's rendering of Loder's beautiful song, *She wore a Wreath of Roses*, which was given with exquisite delicacy and taste'. There is no indication of the writer's identity!

Above left: Drawing of a Brighton College Corps Band uniform, 1860. A French invasion scare resulted in the formation of the Brighton College Volunteer Rifle Corps. It was the first time the College had put any of its pupils into uniform. The Corps consisted of every boy over 4ft 2in in height. There were sixty-six of them and a fife and drum Band of sixteen small boys. Mowbray Gray (1855-62) reported that they were armed with carbines left from the Crimean War and took long marches over the Downs. The Band's limited repertoire included *The British Grenadiers*. Various reasons were given for waning enthusiasm such as parental refusal to replace outgrown (and no doubt expensive) uniforms and the taunts of the local lads. Whatever the cause, the Company had gone by 1869. An original Band uniform was rediscovered in the College in the 1950s and was drawn by K.D. Barnes. It then disappeared again. The drawing is all that remains.

Above right: Maj.-Gen. Sir Herbert Stewart, KCB. He was the first Old Brightonian (1854-56) to be knighted. Like so many Brighton College boys of his generation he chose a military career in which he excelled. He was the commander of a picked force sent to attempt the rescue of Gen. Gordon at Khartoum. Having crossed 150 miles of the Bayuda desert they won a desperate victory at Abu Klea. Two days later Stewart was mortally wounded and died on the 16 February 1885. He was buried in St Paul's Cathedral.

General Sir Harry Prendergast, VC, GCB was another Old Brightonian (1849–50) who became a distinguished soldier. He was born in India but, when his mother died, he was sent to live with his grandparents in Brighton. He was commissioned in 1854 and was posted to the Madras Engineers. During the Indian Mutiny he saw repeated action, was seriously wounded and was twice recommended for the VC. He finally won the bronze cross at Mundisore when he risked his own life to save a fellow officer. In 1885, as commander of the British Burma Division, he carried out a brilliant campaign to depose the king and add Burma to the British Empire. In spite of his undoubted success his military career stalled. He became disillusioned and returned to England. He renewed contact with his old school and served as President of the Old Brightonian Association from 1901 until his death in 1913.

THE BURMESE TOAD.

This cartoon, published in *Punch* in October 1885, celebrated the defeat and deportation of the last king of Burma, Thibaw (then spelt Theebaw), who was barbarous and incompetent. He is portrayed here as a toad. Although Sir Harry Prendergast had been responsible for the king's defeat, the military figure seen in the cartoon kicking the toad was in fact the Viceroy of India, the civilian Lord Dufferin.

Capt. William John Gill (1856–61). He was commissioned in the Royal Engineers in 1864. Having inherited a considerable fortune, he was able to indulge his interest in exploration. After an adventurous journey in Northern Russia he mapped much of Persia and the little-known Tibetan/Chinese border. For this work he was awarded the Founders Gold Medal of the Royal Geographical Society in 1879. He was attached to the Intelligence Department of the War Office and in 1882, during the Anglo-Egyptian War, he was sent into the Sinai Desert and was killed while spying behind enemy lines. His remains were buried in the crypt of St Paul's Cathedral and his sword hangs above his memorial in the College Chapel.

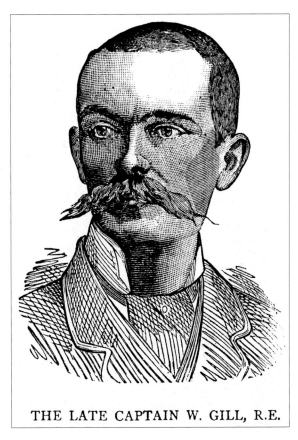

THE LATE CAPTAIN W. GILL, R.E.

Augustus Raymond Margary (1858–65). He, like William Gill, his contemporary at the College, was an intrepid explorer. He joined the Diplomatic Service in China and was awarded the Albert Medal for gallantry in saving life during a typhoon in Formosa (Taiwan). He opened an overland route between China and Burma (1874–75). His murder on the Burmese frontier (known as the Yunan case) led to Britain forcing China to make major trading concessions to British merchants in the 1876 Chefoo Convention. He too has a memorial in the College Chapel.

Victorian School Masters, 1871. From left to right, back row: E.H. Woodward, C.H. Griffith, J.B. Slight, G. Allen, J.T. Wardroper, G.E. Cotterill. Front row: F. Heppenstall, G. Long, The Revd Dr J. Griffith (Principal), J. Newton (Vice Principal).

Four of these later became Headmasters. George Long had been Professor of Ancient Languages of the University of Virginia and then Professor of Greek and also Professor of Latin at University College London. Grant Allen only stayed for a year and later enjoyed brief fame for his novel, *The Woman Who Did*.

Thomas Graham Jackson (1850–53). The distinguished architect in his *Recollections* provided a rich source of information about the very early days of the College. He described how the first Principal was at a disadvantage because corporal punishment was not allowed and the School's reputation was threatened by the frequency of suspensions and expulsions. Much later in his life he claimed, at an OBA dinner, to have been the first pupil to be flogged after a change of policy. He won a scholarship to Wadham College, Oxford and from 1858–61 studied under Sir George Gilbert Scott. Like Scott he built up a formidable reputation. He was created Baronet in 1913 and took over the presidency of the OBA from Sir Harry Prendergast. His last major work was the extension of the College Chapel as the memorial to the dead of the First World War.

The Old Cricket Pavilion, 1882. Gilbert Scott had died in 1877 and thus it was natural for the College to turn to his eminent pupil when the next stage of expansion was planned. His first commission was for the Pavilion which was funded by subscriptions from Old Brightonians whose Association was founded in the same year. The Pavilion very nearly completed its century, but was demolished in the late 1970s to make way for the development of the west side of the home ground. The new building includes a Pavilion, classrooms and the Pre-Prep School.

The two new boarding houses built by Jackson, *c.* 1885. House A on the right, designed to house forty boys, was named Chichester in honour of the College's first President. House B, first occupied by boarders and known as Hampden, was taken over by the Day Boys, *c.* 1893. When they were transferred into the gatehouse in 1895, the Junior School moved in. There they remained until 1918 when House B became Bristol. Both houses were part of the grand design of the 1880s which the Council hoped would transform the small provincial school into a large public school of national (and possibly wider) renown. Jackson's designs were for four boarding houses arranged on either side of a splendid Gate Tower, a Great Hall (Big School) and a new Chapel. The dream of completing the quadrangle gave way to fiscal reality.

Opposite below: The Tuck Shop, 1890s. The earliest Tuck Shop was a mobile affair known as 'Brandy Balls' which featured in the famous cartoon of 1848. The one shown here was in a passage leading to the back quad. It was kept by the Chief Porter's wife, Mrs Howard, known as 'Mother'. At break the scrum for cakes in the narrow space was known as a 'wolley', a word invented by the boys. It was one of only three words peculiar to the College which have survived.

Above: Junior Department Classroom, *c.* 1895. In the early days of the College the younger pupils were taught in the lower forms. In 1882 a separate Department was set up for them in St George's Lodge at the corner of College Place and Eastern Road and two years later it moved to Nos 1 and 2 Walpole Road. There it stayed until it was brought back inside the College into House B in 1895.

Opposite above: The Dining Hall, 1896. This was designed by Gilbert Scott as part of an extension to the Principal's House in 1865-66. At that time there was only one boarding house on the College grounds and the Principal was also the Housemaster. It was known as The House. In addition to the Dining Hall, a Kitchen and a Dormitory Block were built. The Hall remained as a refectory exclusively for the use of School House, as it was named after Chichester and Hampden were created. It was also used for major School functions. It is now the College Dining Hall and the girls of Fenwick occupy what was the Dormitory Block.

Opposite below: The House, 1871. Because it was the only internal boarding house at this time and the Juniors had not yet been separated from the rest, this photograph shows a wide age range. Apart from 'academical dress' for Senior boys, no uniform regulations were imposed until the 1880s. However, the majority of this group are wearing the same type of boater or cap and a few are sporting bowlers.

Chichester House, 1895. From left to right, back row: A.C. Brown, H.P. Crampton, M.C. Kiernander, J.F. Rutter, P.H. Spoor. Second row: A.G. Buhl, J.H. Rutter, R.B. Avern, C.L.A. Smith, E.C. Harrison, C.L. Simpson, C.D. Foster, M.T. Saunderson, R.A. Cullen. Third row: C.S. Young, F.S. Playne, Mr Perrott, Mr Taylor, Mrs Taylor, Miss Skaife (Matron), H.N. Lyle. Front row: G. Willis, D.B. Rose, Joan Taylor, J.L. Taylor, H.W.L. Hobson, B.B. Avern.

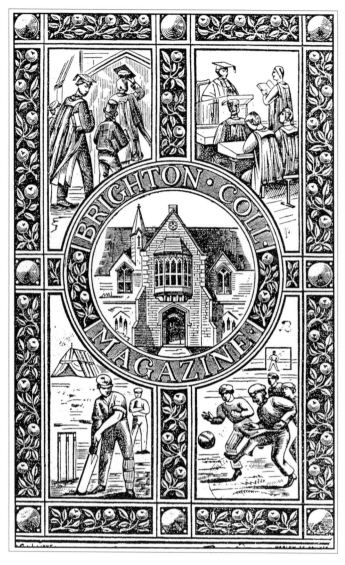

The original cover of the *Brighton College Magazine,* 1869. This
was designed by Sir Thomas Jackson and, without the pictures, it
continued to be used until 1933. The first magazine ever published by
an English school was produced at Brighton College in November
1852. It contained an account of the first three years of the School
by a pupil known as 'T.E.H.' In his *History* G.P. Burstow suggests that
this was probably Thomas Erskine Holland, later Chichele Professor
of International Law at Oxford. The early copies appeared only
occasionally and consisted mainly of articles and poems which had
no connection with the School. In the 1870s, however, the magazine
became a record of College life and from its pages may be gleaned
a fascinating picture of the numerous societies with which the boys
developed their interests and enthusiasms. In the late 1930s the name
was changed to *The Brightonian* and thus it remains.

two

Survival and Expansion
1900-1920

Back from the Brink

The Headmaster at the turn of the century was the Revd Arthur Titherington, (the title of Principal had been changed in the 1880s). He had accepted the post in 1895 fully aware of the parlous state of the College finances. There had been no permanent rise in the numbers on Roll and the Council had had to agree to voluntary liquidation. Titherington had taken on a school owned by the Phoenix Insurance Co. Fortunately for the future of the College he proved equal to the challenge. The Phoenix had insisted that no restriction on admission should continue and the ability to pay fees was to be the only qualification for parents. Together with the broader social intake came the realisation that an urban school short of boarders should encourage Day Boys rather than regard them as inferior. In 1905 a small new block between the Main Building and the Chapel was built for the Day Boys, then known as Hampden House. The Junior Department expanded into the vacated space in the Gate Tower and, in Martin Jones' words, 'proved a lifebelt … during the Phoenix years'. The survival of the College was assured and in 1909 freedom from Phoenix control was finally negotiated by Titherington's more famous successor, the Revd William Dawson (1906-1933).

A War Office letter to the Headmasters' Conference, fears of the growing German army and reports of military weakness in South Africa led to the revival of the Cadet Corps in September 1900. They are wearing their scarlet tunics and dark blue trousers with a narrow red stripe. They were attached to the 1st Volunteer Battalion, Royal Sussex Regiment and took part in the local ceremony to mark the accession of Edward VII in January 1901.

Above: The Corps on parade, 1906–07. The splendid-coloured uniform had been replaced by khaki and membership had become compulsory at the College. By 1907 the *Brighton College Magazine* reported numbers as five officers and 150 rank and file. The following year they were renamed the Officers' Training Corps under the new Haldane scheme.

Right: Lt R.C.B. Henry (1892–95), Royal Dublin Fusiliers, who was the first Old Brightonian to be killed in the Boer War. He fell at Colenso on 15 December 1899. Considerable space in the *Brighton College Magazine* was devoted to OBs on active service and the issue of July 1900 reported the number as forty-eight. A memorial window to commemorate the eight who died in South Africa was unveiled on Speech Day in October 1903.

Because of the evangelical nature of its foundation the Victorian College had viewed drama as immoral. Martin Jones quotes the Revd Henry Venn Elliott (one of the vice-Presidents of the College Council in 1845 and founder of St Mary's Hall) as having considered that theatre and opera, 'risk the everlasting salvation of those who exhibit them'. On Speech Days there had been readings of excerpts from plays and the Reading Club provided opportunities to sample scenes from works by Shakespeare, Sheridan and Goldsmith. No costumes or scenery were allowed. Some staging of extracts was attempted in the 1880s but the first complete work with costumes, scenery and footlights did not appear until Christmas 1900, when *The Yeomen of the Guard* was performed. Sadly, although the *Brighton College Magazine* reported that some excellent photographs had been taken, none survive in the Archives.

This page: The Cyclops of Euripides, December 1903, was the first full play staged at the College. It was performed in Greek. Mr A.H. Belcher (member of staff and future Headmaster 1933-36) played the leader of the chorus and his younger brother, Gordon, was Polyphemus, the Cyclops. (Gordon was the School Captain, later joined the staff and was one of three Belcher brothers to be killed in the First World War). One of the sailors of Odysseus was J.A. Ryle (future Professor of Medicine at both Oxford and Cambridge), and W.M. Malleson the dramatist and actor, was in the chorus of satyrs.

Opposite above: Time Will Tell, a comedy by Herbert Gardner, was performed in December 1905. Mr A.H. Belcher (on the far right) was again in the cast and the *Brighton College Magazine* reported that the boys greatly appreciated his line, 'You can't imagine me playing football'. On W.M. Malleson the reviewer wrote, 'He showed natural dramatic instinct and ability, and remarkable confidence … he should then be a finished character actor'. A very accurate prediction.

Opposite below: The Merchant of Venice, December 1917. Little drama had taken place after the 1905 production and no play had been staged since 1913. Most of the cast were therefore novices and *The Merchant of Venice* was an ambitious choice. It was also a great success. As before, Masters joined with pupils to provide the cast and Mr Lister (nicknamed 'Shotty') was described as a 'tower of strength' in the part of Shylock. After this performance College drama never looked back.

The Library, *c.* 1900. Martin Jones once described it as 'resembling a gentlemen's club'. It was housed on the ground floor of the Main Building. Until 1887 it was also where the College Council met. It was moved to the attics of the Dawson Building around 1930, and, when it was rehoused again around 1960, the attic space became the College Archives.

The Upper West Corridor, *c.* 1900. The College Museum displays can be seen on the left. The Museum had been started in the 1880s by J.H. Davies, one of the Masters, who was already running an entomological exhibition. The Secretary and Bursar, F.W. Madden, presented his collection of electrotype copies of Greek coins, and stuffed birds and geological specimens were added later. In 1904 presentations included a giant frog from the West Indies, a stuffed fox and various snakes, and Mr Thomas rearranged the specimens in both east and west corridors. Later photographs show larger displays on both sides of the corridor.

School House, 1903. The Headmaster, the Revd Arthur Titherington, is seated in the centre behind the cups. He was also Housemaster. The lady to the right of him is his wife who was known affectionately to the boys as 'Mother'. The Matron is seated next to her.

The Old Brightonians' Dinner, June 1903. This event was held in the Empire Hall of the Trocadero, Piccadilly Circus. The Association had been founded in 1882 and was clearly flourishing. The annual subscription a century ago was 5s and an OB blazer cost less than one pound. A section in the *Brighton College Magazine* carried news of activities and sport. The OB Football Club was particularly successful, winning the Sussex Cup every year from 1909 to 1914 and beating all other old boy sides to win the Arthur Dunn Cup in 1913.

The fire at Abbey's Brewery, June 1907. The brewery stood at the corner of Eastern Road and Sutherland Road and the frontage of the College can be seen on the right of the photograph. The *Brighton College Magazine* reported that the boys of School and Chichester Houses and the Junior Department, 'all turned out in force in the small hours of the morning in response to cries of "Fire!"' The malt houses were almost entirely destroyed, but a few broken windows in Chichester House were the sum total of damage to the College. It was very fortunate that the wind had veered to the east only a few hours before the blaze.

New motor fire engine. This recently introduced fire-fighting equipment was used to help put out the blaze at the brewery.

Sir John Murray (1878-79) on the veranda of Government House in Papua New Guinea, which was then an Australian territory (1908). Sir John had been expelled from the College for hitting a Master and in 1886 reached the final of the Amateur Boxing Association Championship of England. He later became a Colonial Administrator.

Judge Murray on circuit, 1908. He held the position of Lieutenant Governor of Papua New Guinea from 1908-1940.

M.J.G Ritchie (1887-88). Tennis had not been played seriously at the College, but Josiah Ritchie reached international fame. Between 1907 and 1910 he was the winner or runner-up at various English, Irish, German and French championships in both singles and doubles. In the 1908 Olympics he won gold in the outdoor men's singles, silver in the outdoor men's doubles and bronze in the indoor men's singles. In 1923, at the age of fifty-three he reached the final of the All England Plate at Wimbledon. He is shown playing at Eastbourne in 1903.

The First XI, 1917-18. This was the very last Association Football season. The game of the 'perfect sphere' had enjoyed great success at the College. The XI of 1909-10 lost only one match and won the Public Schools' Challenge Cup. Among other public schools, however, Association Football was losing support and Brighton changed to rugby, which, in one version of the College football song, had been scornfully referred to as 'the game of the out-grown egg'. From left to right, back row: P.R.D. Spurgin, A.J. Walker-Longley, D.F.A. Apthorp, R.B. Cave, B.R. Bennett, E. Garland. Front row: L.B. Barton, F.R.H. Beven, C.C. Rutherford, M.H. Tollit, R. Nutt.

Just over a century ago in 1906, the College Council made an unconventional decision to appoint the Revd William Rodgers Dawson as Headmaster. There were those who questioned his academic standing. He has remained to this day the only non-Oxbridge man to hold the position. This, however, proved to be of little significance when weighed against the extraordinary effect he was to exert on the future of Brighton College. He had tremendous physical presence and a fascinating personality which worked its magic even on those whom he offended. Parents, staff and boys fell under his spell. He was convinced that God had ordained his appointment. Who therefore could thwart his ambition? He firmly believed he could make the College the greatest public school in England. The numbers on Roll would be the decisive factor and he was, in Martin Jones's view, 'a born recruiting sergeant'. He would accept anyone whose parents could pay the fees. Numbers increased, financial stability followed and the Chief led his School towards the fulfilment of his dream.

The Great Hall, 1914. As finances improved the Phoenix agreed to advance funds for a large School Hall. This had been needed since the College's foundation and had been included in Jackson's plans of the 1880s. Now finally in 1913 the foundation stone was laid by J.M. Cotterill (1865-69), youngest son of Revd Henry Cotterill, second Principal (1851-56). The architect was F.T. Cawthorne and a year later the Earl of Chichester performed the opening ceremony. The west side of the Main Quadrangle was complete. Also in 1914 the main block of College buildings was converted from gas to electricity.

The OTC at camp, July 1914. The camp was quickly struck when news of war came on 4 August. The Headmaster had already spoken to the boys of the duty of their generation to defend their country, and they, like other young men from many walks of life, were prepared for self-sacrifice. The tragic roll of deaths on active service began before August was out. The *Brighton College Magazines* of the war years carried not only the black-bordered Roll of Honour but also the names of the wounded and of all OBs and staff serving in the forces. In marked contrast to what was happening across the English Channel, School routine was barely disrupted. Numbers on the Roll were steadily rising and indeed increased by forty-four per cent from the outbreak of war to 1918. College finances were buoyant. There was little threat of air attack so boys were not withdrawn by anxious parents and food rationing was not introduced until the U-boat blockade started to take effect in 1916-17. Catering became difficult in the boarding houses but the Housemasters' wives coped. Mrs Belcher in Chichester House is said to have queued in all weathers for food for her charges. In 1917 the College rented some land to grow potatoes and other vegetables and two squads of fifty OTC boys went to farming camp in Gloucestershire where their work was much appreciated by the local farmers. College boys also helped to clear snow on Marine Parade when labour was short. The guns of the Somme were heard on the Playground in 1916 but conveyed nothing of the reality of war to the boys. The 12th Battalion, The Sherwood Foresters, made the College their headquarters from Christmas 1914 till the following Easter but caused little disturbance. The greatest threat was that of requisitioning. In October 1916 the Headmaster was told by the Chief Constable that the College buildings had been requisitioned by the War Office. Dawson stormed off to the police station and expressed himself so forcefully that, as a result, other arrangements were made.

Two Old Brightonian War Poets

Francis St Vincent Morris
Second Lieut., Sherwood Foresters,
attached RFC
Born: 1 February 1896
Brighton College, Chichester House, 1910–14
Died of wounds, France, 29 May 1917

THROUGH vast
     Realms of air
          . we passed
On wings all-whitely fair.

   Sublime
On speeding wing
          we climb
Like an unfettered Thing.

   Away
Height upon height;
          and play
In God's great Lawns of Light.

   And He
Guides us safe home
          to see
The Fields He bade us roam.

FRANCE,
     April, 1917.

GHOSTS OF WAR

(SENT FROM FRANCE IN OCTOBER 1917)

WHEN you and I are buried
     With grasses over head,
The memory of our fights will stand
Above this bare and tortured land,
We knew ere we were dead.

Though grasses grow on Vimy,
And poppies at Messines,
And in High Wood the children play,
The craters and the graves will stay
To show what things have been.

Ewart Alan Mackintosh
Lieut., Seaforth Highlanders
Born: 4 March 1893
Brighton College, Hampden House, 1905–09
Killed in action, France, 21 November 1917

The Brighton College War Memorial, which took the form of an extension to the Chapel, completed in 1923. As the number of boys rose, it had become increasingly difficult to seat them in Chapel. It was agreed that enlargement of that building would be a fitting memorial for those OBs who had made the supreme sacrifice in the First World War. An appeal was launched by the OBA and Sir Thomas Jackson was invited to submit a design. His plan was to make the original Gilbert Scott Chapel into the side aisle of a much larger church with a tower, but this had to be scaled down when sufficient funds were not forthcoming. Nevertheless, the enforced simplicity of design in no way detracts from the significance of the enlargement. The names of the dead are carved into the north-west wall without embellishment, a stark reminder of the tragic toll of young lives. Other memorials were added including the stained glass window which bears the names of the three Belcher brothers. The *Brighton College War Record, 1914-19* was published in 1920 and contains details of the war service of all OBs. It has a complete list of all 146 who died and includes portraits of most of them.

The 12th Battalion, The Sherwood Foresters, who had made the College their headquarters for several months before embarking for France at Easter 1915, presented the splendid brass lectern as a token of their gratitude. It can still be seen in the Chapel today.

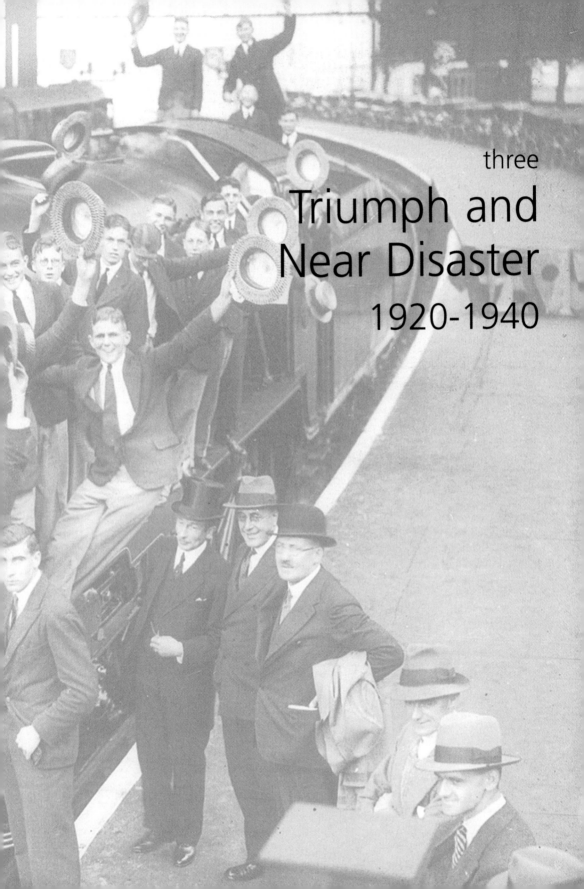

three

Triumph and Near Disaster

1920-1940

Dawson's grandiose plans for the College now moved towards maturity. The policy of expansion continued but, although the desired image of a traditional public school required a predominantly boarding community, the College Council did not provide new accommodation on site. Six boarding houses were set up between 1909 and 1923, Durnford, Walpole, Bristol, Gordon, Wilson and Stenning. Five of them were established in large houses in the neighbourhood, bought or rented by the Housemasters, and Bristol was founded in House B when the Junior Department moved out. By the mid-1920s the College was gaining national recognition. It had acquired an official Coat of Arms and it hosted the Headmasters' Conference in 1926 as a result of its championing of the cause of charitable tax status. An Old Brightonian Masonic Lodge was founded and a new home Mission was launched to the nearby slum parish of St John, Carlton Hill. A register of the first 5,000 old boys was published and Commemoration Day was inaugurated to provide a focal point in the College year. Happily, after a short hiatus, this summer celebration is to be revived in 2007. Team games flourished, the Swimming Pool was opened in 1923 and achievement in sport was crowned by the all-victorious shooting VIII at Bisley in 1927. The royal visit in 1930 for the opening of the new classroom block must have seemed the final accolade. However, Dawson was overcome by events beyond his control. Numbers had already peaked and the dynamic Headmaster, who had succeeded in placing Brighton College on the map, now saw his achievements begin to collapse in the face of the world economic Depression.

The Brighton College Shield.

In 1918 the Council of Brighton College, with the enthusiastic support of the Headmaster, had applied to the College of Heralds for a legitimate Grant of Arms, and on 18 June 1920 the patent was issued. This gave Brighton College its official coat of arms. On a blue background, two crossed golden keys. Above them a closed silver book with golden clasps and edges. At each side a silver pelican facing inwards, wounding its breast, showing red drops of blood. The motto was not included, neither was there a crest, nor supporters.

The crossed keys are the symbol of St Peter, Patron Saint of Brighton, to whom the College Chapel is dedicated. A book in heraldry represents property and stands for the College itself. The pelicans are from the arms of the Earls of Chichester, of whom the fourth, fifth and sixth were the first three Presidents of the College. The pelican in heraldry is always drawn wounding her breast. The old belief was that she used to feed her young with her own blood.

Brighton College Preparatory School in Lewes Crescent, 1919-1940. Following the example of other public schools, it was decided to move the Junior Department outside the School grounds. The Juniors took possession of three rented houses in College Terrace (1918) and the following year they were evicted again to make way for a new boarding house in memory of Gordon Belcher. They were sold off to two College staff (J.H. Arnold and J.M. Gaussen) and moved to Lewes Crescent. They still used some College facilities but, in spite of that and their name, they were basically an independent preparatory school, many of whose pupils did not go on to the College.

Manor Farm playing fields, *c*. 1914. Since games had been made compulsory and numbers were rising, the Playground could no longer provide sufficient space. One of the College Governors, Lord Francis Hervey, obtained a lease on 8.5 acres at Manor Farm behind St Mark's church. The rent was very low and the cost of levelling the ground was met by Lord Francis himself. St Mark's spire can be seen on the right of the picture. The need for extra pitches led the Council to take a temporary lease on land in Whitehawk in 1916 and later they bought and levelled a large ground at East Brighton Park. Burstow tells how College boys of 1925 remembered having to clear loose stones to make the pitches safe for rugby.

The Boxing Club, 1927. From left to right, back row: E.E. Grose, E.W. Browne, R.I.P. Shankey. Middle row: J.K.T. Earle, J.W. Thompson, H.T.T. Holman, C.J.B. Manning, C.E.D. Davy. Front row: M. Ionoff, O.C. Chave.

From 1920 boxing enjoyed a revival. It was part of the Lent term sports programme. A House Challenge Cup was presented by Mr C.E. Spicer and the first boxing competition in March 1920 was won by Durnford House.

The Swimming Pool, designed by F.T. Cawthorne, was completed in 1923. Since Brill's Baths had closed, the Swimming Team had had to travel to Hove Baths when the sea was too rough. With the opening of this indoor heated pool, swimming and water-polo quickly developed. The teams were coached by Howcroft, an international. No fewer than six swimmers from the Dawson era later won half blues as did four at water-polo.

First XI, 1927. Left to right, back row: E.W. Gater, A.R.M. Edwards, J.W. Thompson, J.D. Ronald. Middle row: I.D. MacDonald, J.A.P. Bartlett, J.H. Green, M.G. Saunders, F.C. Jarchow. Front row: T.S. Levett, R.N. Jones, V.H. Hanschell. Cricket failed to see an unbeaten XI in the 1920s but some fine batsmen emerged.

The shooting VIII, 1927. From left to right, back row: Cadet Gorham, Cpl Slearer, Cadet Marshall, Cadet Pickering. Second row: Cadet Young, Cpl Willis, Cadet Junkison, L/Cpl Bond. Third row: R.S.M. Hawkins, Cpl Allen, Sgt Simpson, Maj. Murdoch-Cozens, Cadet Wilson, Q.M.S. Boxall. Front row: L/Cpl Beevers, Cadet Lonsdale. They had returned triumphant from Bisley where they had won all eight trophies, including the coveted Ashburton Shield. This record has never been equalled.

George Morgan Edwardes-Jones, KC (1869-77). Until the 1920s only nine 'Great Schools' (like Eton, Harrow and Winchester) were exempt from tax. All other schools, even if they were registered as non-profit making, were liable to pay. Brighton College first championed the cause of charitable tax status in 1915. The case was led by George Edwardes-Jones, an Old Brightonian. In the high court judgement went in the College's favour but it was defeated on appeal and in the House of Lords. However, the Finance Act of 1927 exempted all registered charities from tax on profits. The Headmasters' Conference gave financial support and in 1926 held its annual meeting at Brighton in recognition of the College's part in gaining such an important benefit for all the member schools.

The Tuck Shop, c. 1930. The old Tuck Shop had become too cramped and in 1921 a large army hut had been erected on the site of the present Art School. The above photograph of a very orderly and well-stocked shop must have been taken in that hut. This temporary building was in its turn outgrown and in 1936 a new tuck and uniform shop replaced it.

Left: Charles Bird Allen, Director of Music, (1921-46). The musical life of the School expanded and flourished under his enthusiastic guidance. He is best remembered for his wonderful productions of Gilbert and Sullivan, which provided the main annual entertainment from 1922-38. They were discontinued as being too expensive in 1939. Allen developed a series of choral groups and broadened the orchestral repertoire to include much that was new and unconventional. He was also responsible for the creation of music practice rooms and in 1938 of two music scholarships. He dominated the musical scene and entertained audiences with conjuring tricks which delighted and sometimes baffled the boys. He was the only recipient of unqualified praise from the inspectors in 1930.

Below: The Sorcerer, 1924. This lesser-known Gilbert and Sullivan was the Christmas production. Unfortunately the photographs were a failure, but the stage manager, Mr W. McCowan, made this drawing of the principal characters.

The Pirates of Penzance, 1936. This was the third production of *The Pirates of Penzance* in the Gilbert and Sullivan series. The *Brighton College Magazine* reported that there were some very strong voices in the cast and some moments of sheer delight. D.J.V. McD. Hobley made his last appearance on the College stage as the Maj.-Gen. and the above picture of his numerous progeny is proof of the skills of Messrs Drury in transforming College boys into such exquisitely dressed ladies.

Euripides' *Iphigenia in Tauris*, 1934. In 1933 Walter Hett (Headmaster 1939-44) produced the first of a series of Greek plays in translation to follow the distribution of prizes on Speech Day. Burstow described them as 'an essential complement to the light-hearted abandon of G and S'. *The Brightonian Magazines* emphasise that scenery, costumes and music were all home-made and all parts were played by the boys. In Jones's words they were 'true school theatre'.

Above: The visit of H.R.H. Prince George (later Duke of Kent) to open the new building, 1930. The photograph shows the royal party leaving the Headmaster's house. Left to right, front row: the Headmaster, Canon Dawson, Prince George of Kent, Mr Wilfred Aldrich (1899-1903), Member of the College Council and Mayor of Brighton. Back row: Lord Daryngton (1881-86), President of the College, an equerry. The Headmaster's family can be seen on the balcony above the front porch.

Speech Day, 1930. The prizes were distributed by the distinguished Old Brightonian (1872-74) Admiral Sir Herbert Leopold Heath, KCB MVO, who is seen on the far left of the group. The others are from left to right: Lady Heath, Mrs Dawson, Canon Dawson.

This rare view shows the marquee set up on the Playground with many parents, friends and boys enjoying afternoon tea after speeches and prize-giving in the Big Hall.

Opposite below: The new block of classrooms, 1930. This block later became known as the Dawson Building. Almost the full cost of construction was raised by an appeal, which was fortunate as numbers had already begun to fall. Designed by F.T. Cawthorne, the new building harmonised perfectly with Jackson's gateway and completed the Eastern Road frontage of the College.

Southern Railway "Schools" Class 4-4-0 Express Passenger Locomotive

Above and below: Naming of the Brighton College Locomotive, 1933. Forty of these magnificent engines were built in the 1930s and were named after leading public schools, including *915 Brighton*. It was placed on exhibition at Brighton Station for the boys to inspect it. All but three of the class were scrapped in 1963. One of the three surviving engines is *928 Stowe* which is the flagship engine of the locomotive collection cared for by the Maunsell Society and based at the Bluebell Railway in Sussex. One of the 'Brighton' nameplates was presented to the College by the railway company and is preserved here in the CDT Department. The other was sold for £3 – the going rate at the time.

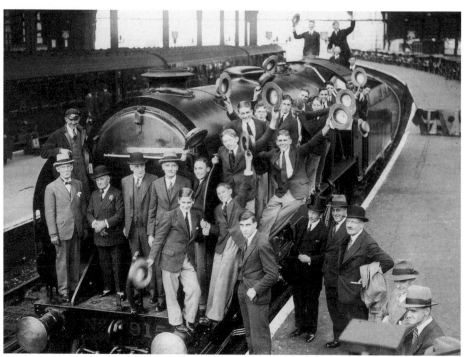

The unsuccessful Everest expedition, 1924. Left to right, back row: Hazard, Hingston, Somervell, Beetham, Shebbeare. Front row: Bruce, Norton, Noel, Odell. Professor Noel Odell (1903-10), geologist and mountaineer. He was Professor of Geology at the Universities of Harvard, Otago and Peshawar, and was a member of the Everest expeditions of 1924 and 1938. He met up again with Capt. John Noel when they were both aged ninety-one. They agreed that spending time at high altitudes in tweeds and clinker-nailed boots and without artificial oxygen did not seem to have done them any harm.

The amateur crew of *Endeavour*, Americas Cup, 1934. Four were Old Brightonians including George Ratsey who won a silver medal for sailing at the 1932 Olympics in Los Angeles. The other three were J.S. Bacon, N.A. Bacon and Walter Richards. They had been near contemporaries at the College around 1920. In 1948 *Endeavour* was the subject of an oil painting by John Worsley, another OB (1932-35). It shows *Endeavour* with 'Tommy' Sopwith at the wheel, racing the American yacht *Rainbow* in 1934. In 1980 Worsley painted a copy which now hangs in the College.

Above: PT in the Front Quad, 1933. A War Office regulation in 1931 raised the minimum age for cadets in the OTC to fifteen. One of the ways of occupying the younger boys after this change was PT, and the beautifully kept lawn in front of the Headmaster's House was an ideal place for this activity. The building in the background is the Convent of the Blessed Sacrament which became the Junior School of Brighton College in 1972.

Below: OTC inspection, date unknown. Gun drill was included for the first time in the annual inspection by Lt-Col. Villiers Smyth, DSO. The post-war rejection of militarism had resulted in a drop in OTC numbers in the early 1920s. However, recovery followed and by 1930 the College contingent was very highly regarded, and an officer and four cadets were invited to parade with the Territorial forces outside Buckingham Palace for the Coronation of George VI in May 1937.

Opposite below: Scout Camp, Bolney, 1938. Left to right, back row: Rayner, Topley, Mr Dencer, Mr Boughton, Mr Stewart, Mr Allen, Pett, Howard, Dr Robertson. Second row: -?-, Mr Lester, -?-.

College scouting continued to flourish but, after the war, it was restricted to the Junior School.

Above: The Jolly Beavers, 1936. Left to right: Anscombe, Topley, Pett, Grose. 'Alf' Lester (staff 1927-1970) described the use of PT for the under-fifteens as 'a soul-destroying time-filler' and started a scout troop in January 1932. Just one year later, the first *Brighton College Magazine* report is proof of its resounding success. The headquarters was in 'an ex-classroom above the porch' which would appear to be the present Library. Friday afternoons were eagerly awaited and a scheme of games and tests, treasure hunts and mock accidents, trips to the Downs for 'wide' games and picnics, occasions such as field day and inspections and, the crowning glory of the year, ten days camp in the New Forest, made sure everyone who joined the troop enjoyed the experience.

R.E. Lester with Senior boys from Wilson's House, 1931. This house at No. 11 Walpole Road was run by the Revd 'Bill' Williams. It gained a tremendous reputation for sport and was Cock House for seven of the fifteen years of its existence. Only four years after this carefree picture was taken, Wilson's fell victim to the economic pressures of the time. Between 1932 and 1935 all but one of the 'new' boarding houses closed. Durnford alone survived the Depression.

A bit of a lark, June 1934. Gwyn Griffiths (1931-34) described how three boys had borrowed dresses from a sister and paraded on the main drive for fifteen minutes before they were spotted by a Master. They fled and were never identified. They could hardly have chosen a more conspicuous location for their escapade.

Right: The Sixth Form Room, *c.* 1935. In the very earliest days of the Gilbert Scott building this room was used as the Chapel. In 1959-60 it became the Library which it remains to this day. During the years in between it was a classroom, and more particularly the Sixth Form Room. One of the double desks survives in the Archives.

Below: The felling of the elms in the drive, 1939. The spread of Dutch elm disease made it necessary to cut down all the elms in the Front Quadrangle. PT squads were used to carry out the sawing and chopping. The sycamore trees were left in situ and lime trees replaced the elms. This drawing appeared in the *Brighton College Magazine*.

School Song.

(FOR a long time the need for a new School Song has been felt. It was with much pleasure therefore that, to meet the demand, the following poem was received from C. V. Hassall whose poetic skill has already several times been displayed on our pages.—*Edd. B.C.M.*)

This is our song that only we may sing,
  We who belong to Sussex and the sea,
Serving one School, at whose demand we bring
  Heart, soul and voice to pledge our loyalty :
Loud be the cry of thankfulness we raise
  For all good things at this our College won,
And louder yet, that men in after days
  May take our theme when we have journey'd on.

Here on the edge of England's utmost hill,
  Here where the winds taste of the salt sea-spray,
Others have learn'd what we are learning still,
  Justly to rule and gladly to obey ;
Mindful of those whose mortal hour is spent,
  So may we win the fight or grandly fail,
Treading ourselves where fearlessly they went
  Under the crest which bears " Let right prevail ! "

Comrades, again our proudest anthem sing,
  Voices of Ocean joining with our own,
While yet we stand in this great gathering
  By the old places where our love has grown.
So to the furthest shores our blessing take
  And echoes of the chorus we have made,
That friendship's bonds here tied may never break
  Nor memories of Brighton College fade.

C.V.H.

The School Song, published 1932. The words were written by Christopher Hassall (1926-30) who has been described as one of the most versatile of Old Brightonians. While he was at the College his poetry helped revive literary contributions to the *Brighton College Magazine*. At Oxford he became an accomplished actor and played Romeo to Peggy Ashcroft's Juliet. He wrote lyrics for Ivor Novello including *Glamorous Nights* and *Careless Rapture* and libretti for Walton's *Troilus and Cressida* and Bliss's *Tobias and the Angel*. He was also the biographer of Edward Marsh and Rupert Brooke.

four

War and
Recovery
1940-1960

Too close for comfort

The need for financial reform had been recognised, but the College had continued to live beyond its means. As early as 1937 a report from Price Waterhouse concluded that the School's very existence was at stake. As war clouds gathered numbers dropped and, after the fall of France in the summer of 1940, the threat of invasion seemed imminent. Brighton was declared a 'defence zone' and the College was the only south-east coast public school not to evacuate or be requisitioned. The new Headmaster, Walter Hett, struggled to maintain numbers and when the lease on the Preparatory School in Lewes Crescent expired, he managed to buy back the School and the Juniors returned to Bristol House and boosted the Roll. The College was saved by the munitions factory and, having survived the worst crisis in its history, it tackled wartime restraints with stoicism. Blacking out all the windows was difficult but not impossible and time-table changes enabled Day Boys to reach home before dark. Cellars and the Hall basement provided shelters and losses of Masters to military service were made up for by bringing men out of retirement and by the employment of the first full-time female member of staff. In spite of victory in 1945 post-war reality was one of continued shortages and rationing. However, austerity meant that private education was one of the few ways people could spend their money. The College also benefited from the abolition of fee-paying places at grammar schools because snobbery motivated parents who viewed free education as an inferior option. The late 1940s saw a healthy rise in numbers.

The Odeon Cinema, Kemp Town, 14 September 1940. There were 1,058 siren warnings in Brighton but only fifty-six were followed by real attacks, mostly hit and run raids. One lone plane released six bombs as it attempted to escape the Spitfire on its tail. The Odeon on St George's Road took a direct hit and a College boy, Peter Stuttaford aged fifteen, who was on duty for the St John Ambulance Brigade at the cinema, was killed instantly. There is a memorial to him in the Chapel. Apart from broken windows and shrapnel in the grounds, the College remained undamaged throughout the war. One precautionary measure involved knocking through the front wall in the south-east corner of the site to provide access for emergency vehicles.

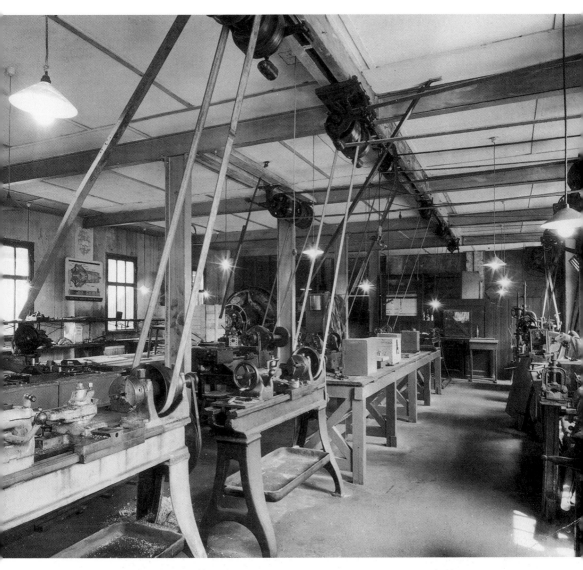

The old Engineering Workshops which became a munitions factory in 1942. This transformation into 'the Engineering Scheme' saved the College in what Burstow described as its 'darkest hour'. By January 1942 numbers had dropped dramatically and Walter Hett, the Headmaster, was determined to resign at the end of the Lent term. The staff were given notice and it seemed that nothing could stop the closure of the School. This third desperate crisis which threatened the College's very existence was averted by the intervention of three men. A parent, Mr George Rushton, ran his own engineering works and was a wartime government contractor. He provided high-quality lathes and placed contracts for die cast and machine tooled components. At Easter work began with thirty-three volunteer Day Boys. A Master, Mr R.E. Lester, was seconded by Hett to run the factory. He taught himself the necessary skills which he passed on to the boys but the high reject rate threatened to ruin the project. This problem was tackled by a Junior House parent, Mr H. Upward, from the Reliance Motor Works. He offered supervision and training, and the reject rate quickly dropped to less than three per cent. Headmaster, staff, pupils and parents volunteered to work two-hour shifts and, under Lester's guidance, the first year earned the College over £2,000. Gradually the financial situation improved.

Left: The Fordson tractor which arrived at the College in June 1941. This enabled Senior boys to join the Ministry of Agriculture's scheme to train tractor drivers, and twenty-six passed the test by the end of that summer term. They then went off to help bring in the harvest in other parts of England. Others went to fruit-picking camps at Horsted Keynes and a farm camp at Mayfield. Boys were drafted off school to pick sugar beet or plant potatoes at Ovingdean. Vegetables were also grown on part of the Home Ground.

Below: The ATC's Avro, 1943. The College had become one of the first schools permitted an Air Training Corps. It was open to boys over sixteen. This was run with great success by the indefatigable Mr Lester, who even made a flight simulator powered by a gramophone motor. The Avro bi-plane was parked in the back quad. In addition to this all boys over seventeen were organised into a Local Defence Volunteer section and, during the Battle of Britain, they guarded the pumping station at Balsdean Reservoir each night against possible saboteurs and German paratroopers.

Above: Charles Fraser-Smith (1915-21). During the Second World War he worked for MI6 and MI9 making gadgets for secret agents. He is seen in the photograph with some of the tricks of his trade — hair-brushes, shaving brushes and golf balls with hidden cavities. Ian Fleming based the character 'Q' in the James Bond stories on him.

Right: Tom Smart, Head Porter, (1925-64). He was a devoted College servant under seven Headmasters. Apparently always cheerful and helpful, he never failed to recognise Old Brightonians when they visited the School. *Burstow's History* includes these words, 'In a world governed by trade union rule Smart would have no place'. In 1945 he was told by the Headmaster, Arthur Stuart-Clark, to ring the School bell 'for a longer time than usual' to celebrate the announcement of VE-Day.

Brighton College, 1945. In a war-weary world the Brighton College Centenary was marked rather than celebrated. This drawing was produced by Miss Freda Sage and it is interesting to compare it with the 1925 view on the frontispiece. The School's War Dead were honoured at Commemoration in 1946. The vellum Memorial Book contains the names of four Masters, 163 old boys and one pupil. It is kept in a glass case in Chapel and a page is turned each week to display different names. In 1997 in a gesture of reconciliation the name of Gunther Guhl (1934-38) was inserted in the book. He served in the German army and was killed in France in 1944. On a shelf above the book stands a Lamp of Maintenance. It was presented in 1922 to a College delegation. Mr Flynn and two Prefects went to the Guildhall for the eighth birthday festival of Toc H. The Prince of Wales made the presentation. The lamp used to be lit for Commemoration. The ritual now takes place on Remembrance Sunday.

74

The Duchess of Kent inspecting the College Guard of Honour at the Royal Pavilion when she visited the town in 1947. The JTC flourished in the late 1940s under a retired regular officer, Lt-Col. Villiers Smyth. In 1949 a Naval section was established and the College was thus able to form a Combined Cadet Force.

Prize Giving, 1948. Left to right: John Sanford, the Headmaster, A.C. Stuart-Clark, Gordon Smith (future College Housemaster and Headmaster of the Junior School), Roy Enfield.

Paris Expedition, Easter 1949. This first post-war trip abroad was organised by Mr M.R. Henderson, Housemaster of Durnford. It proved to have been a great success and the *Brightonian* hoped that it would become an annual event. The photograph was taken by Mr R. Vearncombe, a Master who had returned to the College after several years spent in a Japanese POW camp.

The Fencing Team, 1949. This was the first proper season. Matches fought five: won three, lost two. Left to right, back row: P. Fisher, A.R. Cushman, R.J. Gundry, C.P. Postlethwaite, A.K.S. Harris. Front row: R.H.P. Miller, C. Rubra (Captain). Fencing became popular when coached by a member of the Olympic team, Mr K.G.C. Campbell. He returned from the war and took charge of School House until his untimely death in 1951.

Carol Service, 1949. The photograph was taken between the Choir rehearsal and the arrival of the congregation. The Festival of Nine Lessons and Carols had been introduced to the College by the new Headmaster in 1944 and, from 1947, a large Christmas tree had been placed in Chapel. Stuart-Clark fostered the arts, and the orchestra and house music competition were revived. The Leonardo Cup (1948) encouraged creativity by offering prizes in craft, literature, art and music.

Peter Gough (left) at a reunion, 1998. With him is a fellow former Housemaster, Ken Leighton. In the 1950s College drama flourished under Gough's inspirational guidance. *The Daily Telegraph* in 1958 wrote that his productions showed 'a quality above anything the term school play can conjure'. His wife, Daphne, enhanced the visual effect with amazing costumes created from whatever was available – often very little! Martin Jones described this period of drama as 'a grand experiment in the theatre of the unfamiliar'. Gough's choice of plays was certainly a source of wonder and delight and Gordon Smith, who appeared in three of his productions, remembered the sheer enjoyment of the experience.

The Hypochondriac, 1956. This was a home-made (ie Gough) adaptation of Molière's *Le Malade Imaginaire.* Mr Sickly (left) was played by Stephen Cockburn, who was on the stage for almost the entire performance and to whom 'chief honours' were given by the *Brightonian.*

The Silent Woman, 1951. This comedy by Ben Jonson was reviewed in the *Brightonian* by Miles Malleson (1898-1908) the distinguished character actor and dramatist. He was not only impressed with the production but also thoroughly enjoyed himself.

Top left: Mistress Otter (Timothy Bavin, future Bishop of Portsmouth)

Top right: Captain Otter (Gordon Smith who gave 'a ripe performance' according to the critic).

Hamlet, 1955. The prince (left) was played by Michael Lindsay and Laertes (right) by John Castle (who later made the stage his career). Robert Skidelsky, our present Chairman of Governors, appeared as Reynaldo. A highly amusing write-up described the back stage problems of producing sound effects long before modern technology. On the second night the trumpets and revelry which should have preceded Horatio's words were not forthcoming. He nevertheless asked his question, 'What does this mean, my lord?' As Hamlet began his reply, his words were completely drowned by magnificent noises which were 'a Gough one-man tumult coming off cue'.

The new Art Room on the top floor of the Dawson Building, 1956. An Art Scholarship had been established in 1950 and Gordon Taylor, an inspiring Director (1954-69), raised the standard of painting, drawing and graphics. In 1960 thirty-six boys were entered for O-level and nine for A-level. Art was at last taking wing.

The Library in the attics of the Dawson Building, 1956. It had been housed here since 1930 and was soon to move again into its present home, when the new Science Block freed space in the Main Building.

The Headmaster's Study, 1956. This magnificent room is above the Gateway. The College motto is carved into the stone fireplace and the date of Jackson's building appears above the mantelpiece. The portrait on the wall is of the Rt Revd C.D. Horsley (1917-20), Bishop of Gibraltar (1947-54). It now hangs in the Common Room.

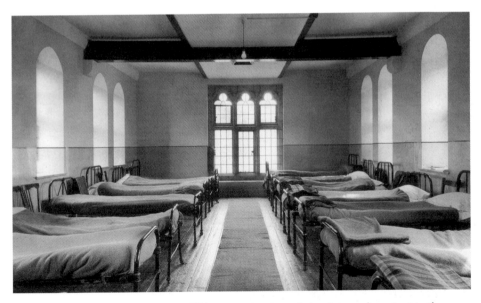

A Chichester House Dormitory, 1956. This spartan accommodation is in stark contrast to the comforts of present-day boarding. The room was unheated but this would have been quite usual half a century ago. An opinion poll carried out in 1957 and reported in the *Brightonian* showed that cold dormitories barely featured as cause for complaint, neither did attendance at Chapel or the length of hair. These would become issues later but, in the late 1950s, the main target was the CCF. Two thirds claimed that they would not join the Corps if it became voluntary.

Old scientific equipment in the Physics Department, photographed in 1994. In the mid-nineteenth century the College had been ahead of its time. There had been an unusual interest in the sciences. The second Principal, the Revd Henry Cotterill, had introduced practical science to the main curriculum in 1852. Chemistry, astronomy, geology, physics and botany were all included. A refracting telescope had been set up and the first purpose-built School Laboratory was erected in 1871. Later this single-storey building east of the swimming Baths was for many years the Music School.

Chemistry Laboratory, late 1930s. These old labs were housed in the upper corridor of the Main Building. When the new Science Block was built in 1958, the space released by the removal of the labs and part of the upper corridor formed the recently-founded Day Boy house, Aldrich. Aldrich has now moved to the refurbished basement of the Hampden/Leconfield building, and the new Sixth Form Centre has taken its place.

Lord Woolton, President of the College, laying the foundation stone of the new Science Building, March 1958. A former maths teacher, he had made his name at the Ministry of Food during the Second World War. There was even a recipe for Woolton Pie to encourage harassed housewives to make the most of their food rations. He was the first really 'hands on' President and, appropriately in view of his wartime position, he overhauled the College Kitchens amongst a great many other contributions during his term of office.

The Headmaster, William Stewart (left) and Sir Vivian Fuchs (1922–26) at the opening of the Science Building, October 1958. Between 1956 and 1958 the College accounts showed a surplus and it became possible to replace some of the worst facilities. The new Science Block was built partly with money raised by an appeal and partly from a grant from the Industrial Fund, set up to help with the cost of building chemistry and physics laboratories in public schools.

The new Science Block, 1958. These new laboratories led to a surge in the numbers studying science in the late 1950s, but William Stewart's Speech Day forecast in 1960 that there would soon be five scientists to every three on the arts side did not become reality. The inspectors in 1961 rated the Science Department as particularly strong, but the arts side held its own. English was 'outstanding' and its Head of Department, Geoffrey Lees, was most highly rated. However, he shared this distinction with Dr John Hall, Head of Chemistry, so honours were even.

The Biology Laboratory in the new block, *c.* 1960. The post-war bias towards maths and science did not develop at the College as had been expected, but blame could not be placed on the facilities after the superbly equipped laboratories had been built.

Dr Vivian Fuchs at the South Pole, January 1958. The distinguished Antarctic Explorer and Scientist led the Commonwealth Trans-Antarctic Expedition, 1955-58. Left to right: Sir Edmund Hillary, Dr Vivian Fuchs and Rear Admiral George Dufek, USN. They continued to Scott Base, Victoria Land where Fuchs received the news of his knighthood. He was awarded the Gold Medal of the Royal Geographic Society in 1951 and its Polar Medal (1953) and Clasp (1958).

The College Kitchens, 1955. The central kitchen had been enlarged and modernised, *c.* 1950. This was one of the projects in which Lord Woolton had had a hand. Part of this work was the provision of a flat above the kitchens for the Housemaster of School House.

The Tuck Shop, 1956. This was combined with a uniform shop and the building had been constructed in 1936. In the early 1970s the Tuck Shop moved yet again to what is now the Blackshaw Room and the Art School and pottery room took over these premises. The Music School next door was enlarged and refitted a few years later.

The School House Dining Hall, 1955. Compare this scene with that of 1896. Formica-topped tables had replaced the sturdy wooden furniture and the starched white tablecloths of a former age. In spite of later refurbishments of the room, Gilbert Scott's superb part hammer-beam and part tie-beam roof (1866) has survived. It even escaped damage in the fire of 1965. The next stage of reform came in 1974 with the ending of formal house dining rooms and the establishment of one central cafeteria Dining Hall in the original School House setting.

Norman Frith entertaining his pupils at the end of term, 1952. This photograph was sent to the Archives by John Miles (1949-52) who wrote, 'I had taken in a pair of plastic spectacles with a false nose attached. Mr Frith, a young man with a sense of humour, donned them for the cameraman'. The three boys are, left to right: Bob Stephens, Mike Senyard and David Downey.

Chichester House, summer term 1953. The Housemaster, W.A. Lloyd, and his wife are seated in the middle of the front row with their three children. The photograph includes three future members of the House of Lords. Robert Alexander is standing immediately behind the Housemaster and his wife. Timothy Bavin is seated at the end of the front row, right. Robert Skidelsky is seated on the ground, far right. The photograph was donated to the Archives by Simon Lanyon, back row, seventh from left.

View of the Main Building through the Gateway, 1956. The two boys in the foreground are
R.C. Usherwood (Head of School) and A.C.S. Carter (Prefect). The boaters which they are carrying
were finally abolished in 1969.

During the 1950s sport flourished, the CCF broadened its programme of activities and the cultural life
of the College reached new heights. The world was changing but the old certainties were still strong and
William Stewart, looking back, reflected that 'Headmastering had been such fun in the 50s'.

five

Challenge
and Response
1960-1980

By 1966 Day Boy numbers had increased to fifty per cent of the School and continued to rise while the number of boarders declined. Durnford became a Day Boy House in 1970, Ryle House was founded for Day Boys in 1979 and in 1983 Bristol closed. The main additions to fabric and facilities are dealt with in the chapter as is the admission of girls in 1973. This surely was the most momentous change in the history of the School. Philip Burstow in his journal in 1969 was convinced the College was falling apart. Society was changing, it is true, and the challenge to authority and to traditional values had been growing since the 1950s. Within the College, however, the symbols of public school life remained and there was no sign of their becoming voluntary. The Corps, the Chapel and cricket were impervious to protest. Many of the boys were restless. Some may even have dreamed of manning the barricades. Nothing of the kind actually occurred. Some remained silent in Chapel, others walked out of meals and one house attended meals but refused to eat. The length of hair became an issue. Sixth formers were now legally adults and the increasing number of Day Boys meant that Housemasters were less able, in Peter Points' words, 'to keep the School ring fenced'. The College weathered the storm and gradual changes were introduced. The atmosphere became less formal, options were offered in sport and a wide variety of activities developed. A Sixth Form Club was established which served beer and a special house was opened in St George's Lodge for the third year sixth, where they did not have to wear uniform. Music, drama and art were encouraged and the curriculum broadened.

Dixon of Dock Green opening the School Bazaar, 1960. Jack Warner, the avuncular character actor, became a nationally recognised figure from his role in the longest-running police series in television history. His opening words in every episode passed into daily usage – 'Evenin' all'. A large number of people visited the College and Mr Warner faced a formidable queue of autograph seekers. Well over £2,000 was raised for the College Building Fund.

New Workshops and Day Boy Houses, 1959-60. The demolition of the old laboratories and the engineering workshops of Second World War fame followed the opening of the Science Block in 1958. New Carpentry and Metal Workshops were built and Hampden and Leconfield were provided with accommodation on the two floors above. Expansion of the towns of Brighton and Hove since the war had ensured the growth of Day Boy numbers and, by 1960, they provided nearly half of the pupils on Roll. Even Stewart could not ignore them and consequently their status rose.

The visit of the Duke of Norfolk, March 1960. The Duke was clearly in a jocular mood and Lord Woolton and the boy snooker player appreciated his humour. His Grace was visiting the new Day Boy Houses after performing the official opening.

The visit of HM the Queen and HRH the Duke of Edinburgh, 1962. It was with great pride that the College welcomed the Queen and the Duke. Excited rows of boys lined the paths as the royal couple were given a guided tour. The Headmaster, William Stewart, is seen here presenting Tom Smart, the Head Porter, to Her Majesty. The Duke of Edinburgh is watching from the porch and Peter Gough, Second Master, is standing behind on the left. The Queen unveiled a plaque which commemorates her visit. It can be seen on the outside of the east wall of the Chapel.

The Library, *c.*1960. A fine new Library was created in the Main Building. This was far more accessible and attractive than the Dawson attics. In 2003 an extension and complete refurbishment provided the College with the superb resource centre we have today.

School House fire, 1965. Norman Frith, the Housemaster, standing in the burnt out ruins. He had slept through the alarm and was the last to know of the trouble. Peter Perfect, the house tutor, had failed to summon the brigade by dialling 000 in the dark. Nevertheless he did contact them and they arrived within five or six minutes and quickly had the fire under control. The boys, well drilled in escape routes, reached the Headmaster's Lawn and assumed that it was yet another sign of their Housemaster's efficiency – a practice at half-past four in the morning! The Study Block, known as Tin Pan Alley, had to be demolished and thus the opportunity arose for a new School House. It is now occupied by the girls of Fenwick.

Above: Molière's *Le Bourgeois Gentilhomme*, 1966. For his final production at Brighton College Peter Gough chose an ambitious double bill. Sophocles' *Oedipus Tyrannus* was a moving performance played against a sombre background of a Greek temple façade. It created a palpable sense of foreboding. In contrast the light, bright stylised set for the Molière comedy drew applause. Mrs Gough had surpassed herself with the costumes and the whole evening was a fitting ending to nearly twenty years of splendid drama.

Above and right: Son et Lumière, 1967. A re-creation of the School House fire provided the dramatic opening of this production. Then the history of the buildings was told in flashback up to the construction of the new School House which symbolised the future. It was an extraordinarily ambitious project, but the combination of voices heard in both words and music and the lighting effects must have formed a remarkable spectacle for those fortunate enough to have shared the experience. It was written and produced by Gordon Smith.

Opposite below: The Glee Club recording the Epilogue, 1965. A section of the Choir was invited to the Southern Television Studios at Southampton to record a week's programmes. The series was called *School Song* and took the form of Epilogues. The theme was humility. The Chaplain, the Revd Bill Peters, who took the service, is standing on the right. Jack Hindmarsh, the director of music, is conducting on the left. A festival of music, art, film and literary activities was organised at this time by Gavin Henderson (1961-65) who later became Artistic Director of the Brighton Festival.

Tickets are now available

for

BRIGHTON COLLEGE
Son et Lumière

an adaptation of the history of the College for voices and lighting effects.

The part of the Chairman of the Council through the years will be spoken by

MICHAEL HORDERN (O.B.)

The Headmaster, The Chaplain, Mr. William Stewart, Mr. Peter Gough, and others, including Tom Smart, will also take part.

The script is by
Mr. GORDON SMITH, assisted by Mr. BURSTOW

Performances are on . . .
Friday, 21st July, until **Tuesday, 25th July**
. . . at 9.45 p.m.

The performances on Friday and Saturday (Speech Day) are reserved for Parents and Old Boys.

Please apply for tickets, at **10/- each,** to
N. J. FRITH, The College, Brighton 7.

A College Pop Group, 1966. The phenomenon of the Beatles had spawned thousands of imitators dreaming of stardom. The College was not immune.

Part of a Sussex University demonstration staged to coincide with the CCF Inspection, 1970. The houses shown here have long since been demolished, but they stood immediately opposite the College in Eastern Road. The banners naturally caught the attention of the press, but the headlines were misleading. The action for which six boys were suspended amounted to about three-quarters of the cadets parading inside the grounds minus a *single* item of uniform. This was the extent of their protest against compulsory membership of the Corps. Schoolboy rebellion did not become revolution.

The Kemp Town Brewery, 1967. This building stood on the corner of Sutherland Road and Eastern Road and adjacent to Chichester House. When the College was founded the Council had been unable to agree terms to purchase this piece of land in the south-west corner of the site they wanted. In 1967 they finally managed to buy the Malthouse for £20,000. A new appeal was launched the following year for an ambitious scheme to provide classrooms, Music and Art Departments, Squash Courts and a Gymnasium on the Maltings land.

The Woolton Building, opened 1972. The original plans had to be scaled down for lack of funds, but the new classroom block included a Lecture Theatre, a Squash Court (now the Rose Lecture Theatre) and a Sixth Form Club. It has recently been announced that a Visual Arts Department is to be located above the Woolton Building. It will be named after the late Lord Alexander of Weedon (1950-55), past President of the College.

The demolition of the Tin Huts, 1972. They were built in the summer of 1920 and used as classrooms M, N, O, P, Q, R and S continuing the sequence A-L in the Main Building. In the late 1930s they were converted into two Day Boy houses, Hampden A and B, later Hampden and Leconfield. Since the opening of the new houses in 1960 the huts had been used as storerooms and a groundsman's workroom. They were originally First World War army huts and did good service for over half a century. They were demolished to make way for the Sports Hall.

The Sports Hall, 1973. William Blackshaw was appointed Headmaster in 1971 and by the time he retired he had become known as 'Bill the Builder'. He certainly made his mark on the fabric of the School. The provision of indoor sports facilities was a major improvement and was made possible by a most generous gift to the College from his mother and step-father, Sir Thomas and Lady McAlpine. A completely new physical activity was introduced by the creation of a climbing wall at the southern end of the Sports Hall. It can be seen in the photograph.

The bridge across Eastern Road, 1970-72. The Juniors had been brought back into Bristol House in 1940 to boost the Roll but, as the danger of enemy action ended and the 1944 Education Act took effect, numbers rose and the College needed the accommodation. The War Office withdrew from Arlington House and Durnford re-opened there. The College bought the former Deaf and Dumb Asylum across Eastern Road and housed the Juniors in its very run-down premises. After twenty-five years a bridge was built to enable the boys to cross over directly into the College grounds. It was only used for two years, as the Juniors moved yet again, but to a vastly superior building. The old Junior School on the right of the photograph was demolished and sheltered housing was constructed on the site (Danny Sheldon House).

The opening of the new Junior School in Walpole Lodge, 1972. The Convent of the Blessed Sacrament decided to sell Walpole Lodge and the Sisters returned to their mother house at The Towers, Upper Beeding. They too had been affected by changes in secondary education. The College bought the Convent School and it became Brighton College Junior School. The picture shows Colin Cowdrey, the celebrated cricketer, performing the opening ceremony. Gordon Smith, who had been appointed Headmaster of the new School, is on the left. The name was changed to the Preparatory School in the late 1990s.

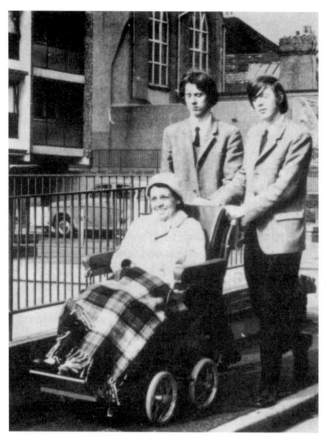

Left: Voluntary Service Unit, 1972. Paul Campbell and Andrew Elliott taking Mrs Boulton out shopping. The unit carried out a wide variety of work and was an alternative to the CCF in the Sixth Form.

Below: Fenwick House, 1979. Probably the most significant event of this period was the arrival of the girls. They were first admitted to the Sixth Form in 1973. A decade later they joined the Junior School and in 1988 the College became fully co-educational. Most were boarders and lived in an 'outhouse' under the supervision of the Chaplain and his wife, Peter and Geraldine Hamilton. As numbers rose David and Stella Grigor took over the house. They became known as Fenwick House, named after a former Matron, and finally in 1983 they moved into School House when the boys went across the quad to the old Bristol accommodation. Richard and Isobel Willmott ran the house with Gill Tissier as House Tutor.

Open Day, 1977. Part of the move towards a less formal approach was the replacing of Speech Day with Open Day. Parents and friends were able to move around the School as they wished and to see not only exhibitions but also lessons and rehearsals in progress. This picture shows the Art Department with painting, drawing, sculpture and pottery on display.

Open Day, 1977. The College Press in action. The young operative has a very attentive and admiring audience. Martin Jones described the press as 'vigorous' and their output at this time was both inventive and impressive.

The new building, c.1980. This formed the completion of the west side of the College site. The much-loved old Cricket Pavilion was demolished. The Council had bought (1971) a pre-prep school, Kingscliffe, based on Eastern Road. The new building provided a Sports Pavilion, a purpose-built home for Kingscliffe (later Brighton College Pre-Prep) and seven extra classrooms for the Senior School.

Opening of the new building, 1980. The opening ceremony was carried out by Lord Denning, Master of the Rolls, who unveiled a plaque in the entrance hall, and the Bishop of Chichester dedicated the building. Left to right: the Bishop, Lord Denning, Mr William Blackshaw, the Headmaster.

six

Sesquicentenary
1980-2000

When Bill Blackshaw had been appointed in 1971 the Council was looking for someone who would 'take the school by the scruff of the neck'. Four boys were expelled and six Juniors beaten in his first ten days. LSD had been involved and clear and decisive action was needed. It certainly worked. Applications took a sudden up-turn. His brief was to raise numbers and by the time he retired in 1987 he had increased the Roll by forty-four per cent. He had overseen the admission of girls to the Sixth Form and agreed that they should now enter at the age of thirteen. However, although he supported the decision he did not feel able to implement it. John Leach took over in 1987 and the following year the College became fully co-educational. In 1990 a new day girl house was opened and in 1995 the College celebrated the 150th anniversary of its foundation. John Leach's brief was to raise academic standards and as Jones reported in 1995, 'they have never been higher'. He added, 'Pupils are kept incredibly busy and competition thrives'. In 1997 Anthony Seldon, the new Headmaster, hit the ground running and never stopped.

Philip Burstow (1924-29). Those who remember Philip Burstow will know of his lifelong devotion to the College both as a boy and a Master. In 1929 he joined the staff of Brighton College Preparatory School in Lewes Crescent and remained in what later became the Junior School until his death in 1975. He was Second Master from 1945 and inspired generations of schoolboys with his enthusiasm for history and cricket – he ran the Junior School First XI for thirty-five seasons. With M.B. Whittaker he wrote *A History of Brighton College*, published in 1957. It was he who saved so many valuable historic papers from the boilers, having been warned of impending disaster when some of his young charges showed him items picked up from the ground in the ! The material he rescued was carefully sorted and put in the Archives which he instituted.

Above: Picasso and the Theatre
Exhibition, 1982. After Philip Burstow's
death Bill Blackshaw was responsible for
the creation of the Art Gallery in the
foyer of the Great Hall in collaboration
with Fred Hankins (director of activities)
and Nick Bremer (director of art). It was
named the Burstow Gallery and over the
years it has provided a setting for a wide
variety of exhibitions and given pupils
an invaluable opportunity to experience
superb painting and sculpture within
their own school. The Picasso Exhibition
extended into the Great Hall and was
the central event of that year's Brighton
Festival. It attracted 7,200 visitors and the
publicity was described as 'beyond price'
by the Headmaster.

Right: The Marriage of John and Fiona
Aiken (*née* Heald), 1983. This was a
very special occasion because they were
the first Old Brightonian couple to
marry. Both their sons have attended
the College. The elder, James, is in his
final year at Leeds, reading history. The
younger, Thomas, is in the Lower Sixth.
He is hoping to read Classics at Oxford
and is also aiming for a rugby blue.
Fiona is the administrator of the OBA.

Above: John Ridler as the Lord Chancellor in *Iolanthe*, 1982. This was a highly successful G and S production by Richard Willmott and Stephen Hicks. To the left of the Lord Chancellor is Aidan Cruttenden who played Lord Tolloller and whose mother was responsible for the splendid costumes.

Left: Salad Days, 1990. The sheer enjoyment of the cast was commented on in the *Brightonian*. Sarah Hanson and David Farnsworth played the central characters with considerable flair. The photograph shows Graham Miller as the cardinal and Graeme Tickner as the bishop. Their antics on stage nearly brought the house down. Moments to be relished were provided by the dons' chorus. Led by the Headmaster, sixteen members of the academic staff strutted their stuff to the delight of the audience. This memorable performance was created by Martin and Jenny Jones with music directed by Stephen Hicks.

Above: The Lester Building under construction, 1985-86. This new block was named after Mr R.E. Lester who had saved the School through his organisation of the munitions factory during the Second World War. It provided new classrooms, an Electronic Laboratory and two Computer Rooms. Only the centre arch is still a thoroughfare as the other two now feature the Bookshop and the Uniform Shop.

Right: The retirement of Bert Swarbrook, (1964-88). He had succeeded Tom Smart as Head Porter and their long and loyal service to the College is commemorated by the engraving on the stone fireplace in the entrance hall of the Main Building. Until quite recently that fireplace was part of the enclosed Porters' Lodge. Bert was in his turn succeeded by Reg Spicer. Now we have a security team who are based in the refurbished original porters' lodge by the Gateway on Eastern Road.

Above: Queenscliffe School, 1980-83. When she had established her Kingscliffe boys in the new Sutherland Road building Mrs Racster, the Headmistress, returned to her old establishment on the corner of Eastern Road and Bellevue Gardens, there to found Queenscliffe for eight to eleven-year-old girls. It flourished for three years but, inevitably, could not continue when the Junior School became co-educational. Mrs Racster retired and Margaret Hollinshead set up Hawkhurst Court, the dyslexic unit, in the vacated girls' school.

Opposite below: Choir Trip to Berlin, 1990. The Choir are seen here in front of the Headmaster's Porch dressed in splendid deep red gowns, prior to their departure for Berlin. They had already sung on *BBC South Today* and *Radio Sussex* and they were confidently setting out, one year after the Berlin Wall began to collapse, to break down any remaining barriers between East and West. They sang in English and German and their venues included homes for the elderly and the handicapped, the Berlin equivalent of Harrods and, the highlight of the week, the Petruskirche, where they received a standing ovation.

Above: Williams House, 1990. This is a purpose-built house for Day Girls sited on the east boundary of the College just south of the side gate on Walpole Road. It was named after Mrs Peggy Williams who was born in Chichester House in 1896 when her father was Housemaster. She married the Revd Bill Williams, Chaplain, and they ran Wilson's House in Walpole Road. The opening ceremony was carried out by Carol Barnes, the television news presenter. Left to right: Canon Peters, who blessed the building, the Headmaster, John Leach, Peggy Williams and Carol Barnes. The first Housemistress was Gill Tissier.

Elgar's *The Dream of Gerontius*, 1991. Stephen Hicks (far left) is seen conducting the final rehearsal for the Choral Society's performance at St Mary's Church, Rock Gardens. Over the years the Music Department, for different works, combined with St Mary's Hall, Roedean or Brighton and Hove High School in its annual concerts. The Choral Society, as it still does today, welcomed staff, parents and friends to join the pupils. The main concert of the year in May is part of the Brighton Festival. It has taken place in various Brighton churches including St Bartholomew's and St George's, Kemp Town. St Mary's was chosen in 1991 because its huge apse could accommodate the 250-strong chorus.

The Three Sisters by Anton Chekov, 1991. Left to right, back row: Sarah Hanson as Natasha, Piers Rennie as Ivan Chebutykin, Luke Johnson as Vassily Solyony, David Gold as Alexander Vershinin, Philip Tredinnick as Fyodor Kulygin. Middle row: Paul Gardener as Andrey Prozorov, Victoria Thomas as Olga, Nicole Streak as Masha, Patricia Harris as a maid. Front row: Christopher MacGregor as Baron Tusenbach, Anna Carne as Irina. The play was produced by Simon Smith and Philip Robinson. Robert Wilmot in *The Brightonian* described it as 'a great performance'.

The Senior Public Speaking Team, 1993. They won the final of the English Speaking Union area competition. From the left: David Salbstein won the salver for the personality of the area final. Attila Malta won the prize for the best Chairman in the Rotary competition. Oliver Willmott won the cup for the best individual speaker for proposing the vote of thanks. The best individual cup had been won in previous years by David Farnsworth, Ralph Oliphant-Callum and David Gold.

'Flying Druids' parachute Jump, 1992. From left to right: Ian Archer, Sophie Ghazal, Simon Smith and Roger Ganpatsingh present a cheque to the Deputy Fund-Raising Manager at Great Ormond Street Hospital following their sponsored parachute jump. The full team numbered sixteen and they spent a day at the Headcorn Parachute Club in Kent. They were given rigorous training and everyone landed safely. This was only one of many fund-raising activities for a wide range of charities in that particular year.

Duke of Edinburgh gold awards, 1994. Helena Green (left) and Beatrice Miller were the first gold award winners at the College for some years. They are seen here attending the county ceremony in Hastings. Later they went to St James's Palace for the formal presentation before the Duke of Edinburgh. The award scheme is still enthusiastically followed, and the number of participants increases each year.

Pilgrimage to the Holy Land, 1993. This group was led by the Revd Paul Hunt who had been head of religious education at the College and had been ordained deacon the previous summer. He is third from the right, standing. We stayed in the hostel attached to St George's Anglican Cathedral in Jerusalem and spent a week visiting the holy places of Christendom and other sites of historical significance. The Headmaster brought back an olive wood cross which was placed on the wall in the Chapel near the door to the vestry. It commemorates an unforgettable experience.

The Service of Thanksgiving for 150 years of Brighton College, 28 January 1995. The Bishop of Chichester presided and the Right Revd David Connor, the Bishop of Lynn, preached to a full congregation at St Peter's, the Parish church of Brighton. The service marked the beginning of a series of events to celebrate the College's Sesquicentenary. It was also a time for reflection on the faith in which the School had been founded and on which its ethos was based.

The opening of the Hordern Room, 29 January 1995. The Chapel Music Room had been transformed into an elegant space suitable for drama, chamber music and many other activities. The Headmaster spoke about Sir Michael Hordern's life, beginning with his schooldays at Brighton College (1925-30) where his interest in drama began, and moving on to his long and versatile career as an actor of stage, screen and television. Sir Michael, clearly moved by the occasion, gave a short speech of thanks and unveiled the bust of himself by Peter Webster and presented to the College by David Land. Sadly our honoured guest died the following May.

As You Like It, 1995. This Shakespearian comedy was the choice made by Simon Smith for the major production of the anniversary year. This proved to have been an admirable decision. A quartet under the direction of David Ollosson provided the music and the cast, the costumes and the set combined to create a memorable evening. At the centre foreground of the picture are Audrey, played by Jo McLennan and Michael Flexer as Touchstone. Philip Robinson in his review described Audrey as 'spectacularly unseemly'. In spite of his reduced mobility, he was intent on also attending the final performance. What more reassuring accolade could there be for a producer?

Opposite below: Alice in Wonderland and *Alice Through the Looking Glass*, 1995.

This was the main event in the Junior School's celebration of the 150th Anniversary of the College's Foundation. It seemed fitting to perform this Victorian fantasy to mark the occasion. Lewis Carroll's children's classic was written when Brighton College was in its infancy and, just as 'Alice' has proved to be of enduring delight to children of all ages, so Brighton College has influenced many generations of children and has shown itself to be of lasting worth.

These words were written in 1995 for the *Brightonian* and it feels apt to repeat them now. Alice was played by Jo Wicks whose performance was a *tour de force*.

Above: The Victorian Fete, 1995. The College made a perfect background for the colourful Fete organised in the summer term. It was opened by Victoria Worsley-Lyon who appeared in a vintage motor car escorted by Michael Flexer. The young children dancing in a ring on the Headmaster's Lawn were on the cover of the *Brightonian*. A brass Band provided music and anachronistic barbecues were tended by men attempting to look like Victorian waiters.

The retirement of Reg Spicer, Head Porter, 1989-97. He is surrounded by three Headmasters.
From left to right: John Leach, Bill Blackshaw and Anthony Seldon.

John Major's visit, 1998. Anthony Seldon was not only Headmaster of Brighton College. He is
a distinguished historian, author, journalist and broadcaster. He had contacts with a wide range
of personalities and the School benefited from these 'outside' interests by having a seemingly
unlimited choice of visiting speakers. These included Douglas Hurd, Dame Stella Rimmington,
Kate Adie and George Melly, to name but a few. The Headmaster had written the authorised
biography of John Major and the former Prime Minister is seen here with pupils left to right:
Chloe Blackburn, Pranay Sanklecha and Charlotte Woodward.

seven

A Changing World

2000-2007

This chapter differs from the others because it covers the very recent past and the present. The twenty-first century presents a challenge to everyone, but especially to young people to whom opportunities rarely offered before are now there for the taking. The Headmaster recently described the world of the College as kaleidoscopic and I have tried to find images which convey at least some impression of this amazingly vibrant community. We are all privileged to be part of a school where everyone is valued and where, as we look to the future, we never forget the thousands who have been here before us and who have helped to make the College what it is today.

Anthony Seldon, Headmaster 1997–2005. This high-profile Headmaster led his School into the new millennium, and future historians will certainly regard his period of office as a most significant chapter in the History of the College. His dynamic personality quickly impressed itself on staff, pupils and parents and his ubiquitous presence reassured us all that the man in charge was in our midst. Nothing escaped his notice and he knew exactly what he wanted to achieve. His success was proved by the impressive legacy he handed on when he departed for Wellington.

The Performing Arts Centre, 2000. This was officially opened by Mr Neville Abraham (1950-55) whose generosity had made the whole scheme possible. The new facility transformed the wind-swept back quad and provided music rooms and a superb dance studio. On the ground floor the Café de Paris is a meeting place for the whole School community and the piazza is enhanced by the water feature.

The BCFS South Downs Way Walking Party, 1998. One of the new Headmaster's first creations was the Brighton College Family Society. He wanted families to enjoy their connection with the School: 'parents, grandparents, friends – everyone is welcome'. An amazingly wide selection of activities is on offer and there is no doubting the popularity of this venture.

Two victims of terrorism

Robert Eaton (1977–80). Robert was a chorister at St Paul's Cathedral before coming to the College. He was also a talented cellist. He was killed in the terrorist bombing of the World Trade Centre on 9/11. He was working for Cantor Fitzgerald near the top of the North Tower. Although he lived and worked in New York he remained an enthusiastic supporter of Brighton and Hove Albion. A minute's silence was held before the first match after his death and a tribute appeared in the match programme.

Daniel Braden (1987–92). Dan attended the Junior School and the College and became head of Ryle House and Deputy Head Boy. He read Mandarin at Edinburgh University and then became marketing manager for a firm in Taiwan. A keen rugby player he was on an end-of-season tour with his club, the Taipei Baboons, and was killed in the Bali bombing of 2002. His parents set up the Daniel Braden Reconciliation Trust called 'Encompass' to promote understanding between peoples of different cultures.

Departing from School, 2005. This painting was the work of Charlotte West and hangs over the fireplace in the Reception Hall of the Main Building. *The Good Schools Guide* recently named the Art Department as the best in the United Kingdom. The new Visual Arts Building will provide even better facilities.

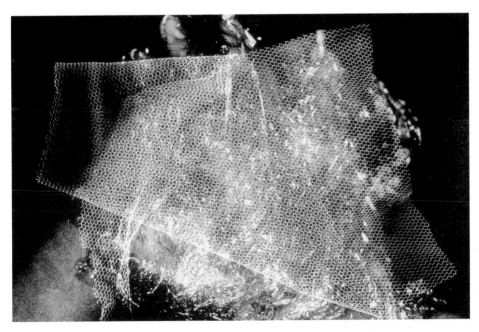

Photograph from Exhibition of A/S work, 2003 taken by Asako Chiba whose untimely death from cancer destroyed a shining artistic talent.

Worli, 2004. It is over twenty years since John Spencer began the connection with the two shanty towns of Mumbai. The College has maintained the link and our sponsorship helps to alleviate the poverty and squalor. Cricket teams and Old Brightonians have visited and the Revd Saba Renjithan and his son the Revd Paul, who have dedicated their lives to their people, greatly appreciate both the financial help and the friendship established between them and Brighton College. The Extra Cover charity in the School has raised over £100,000 for tsunami relief in Sri Lanka. The Romanian orphanage project, set up by Conrad Sandercock in the early 1990s, continues every year with a group of staff and pupils visiting Slatina to carry out a wide variety of useful tasks. Jane Langhorne now leads this venture.

St Joseph's Rugby Festival, 2006. Brighton College's First XV Rugby Captain, Ryan Manyika, was named player of the tournament at the National Schools' Festival in Ipswich. This award is one of the most prized in schoolboy rugby. Ryan scored the most tries in the entire tournament and was praised for his flair and creativity in heading his team. Centre of picture, left to right: Ryan Manyika and Thomas Aiken.

Right: Clare Connor, OBE, 2006. Clare attended the Junior School where her early interest in cricket was encouraged by James Mackintosh, and the College (1989-94) where, under the guidance of John Spencer, she was the first girl to play for the First XI. She later became Captain of the England Women's Team which won the Ashes in 2005. She has now retired from the international scene but teaches English at the College and is involved with girls' cricket. The Clare Connor Scholarship has been won by three girls – Holly Colvin, Laura Marsh and Sarah Taylor – all of whom have been selected to play for England.

Below: Girls' Netball, 2000. Old Brightonian Netball VII v College First VII. Left to right, back row: Lucy Chapple, Clare Frances, Carly Shackleton, Corrie Pope, Elizabeth Jones, Melanie Ford, Kathryn Lowe, Samantha Halpin. Middle row: Kerry Ford, Helen Hopson, Charlotte Allen, Kate Burton. Front row: Candice Brackpool, Katy Enright, Anna Lines.

Left: One Montague Place, 2002. This five-storey converted Chapel in Kemp Town provides facilities for music, drama and English as a second language. The building was bought by the Scholarship Trust and was formally opened by Robert Seabrook, Q.C., Chairman of Governors, Professor Paul Robertson of the Medici Quartet and Ralph Allwood, Musical Director of Eton College.

Below: The Chamber Choir outside St George's Chapel, Windsor, 2004. This is a specialised choir with a wide repertoire of sacred and secular music. They have sung evensong at St George's Chapel and at St Paul's, Southwark, Chichester and Portsmouth Cathedrals. In 2005 they went on tour to Prague and hope to go to Moscow this year.

National U17 winners, Chamber Music Competition, 2004. In the finalists' concert at St John's, Smith Square, London the quartet played the *Requiem for three cellos and piano* by David Popper. Left to right: Sandy Chenery (Deputy Director of Music), Rosie Goddard, David Tregenza, Rachel Varughese, Rain Wu, Eleanor Whipple (Head of Strings), Richard Niblett (Director of Music).

Dance, 2007. Since the opening of the PAC, dance has enjoyed considerable success. Over 150 pupils are members of the Dance School and the subject is studied at GCSE, AS and A-levels. The highlight of the year is the show at the Gardner Arts Centre on the University of Sussex campus. The two dancers above are Emily Thomas and Andrew Hardwidge.

Oxbridge Record, 2007. Sixteen pupils have been offered places at Oxford and Cambridge. This is the highest number ever. Left to right: Raymond Li, Matthew Commin, Betty Gration, Toby Brown, Rachel Varughese, Alex Sobolev, Charlotte Hogg, Anthony Cheung, Kathryn Hopwood, Andrew Donner, Abigail Lappo, Christopher Waite. Those not in the photograph are Tamzin Merchant, Jon Monk, Alastair Sava and Roland Singer-Kingsmith.

The *Brightonian*, 2005-06. The *Brighton College Magazine* has become a full-colour, large format production which includes details of all three Schools. Last year's cover featured Damon Kerr's spectacular musical extravaganza *On the Town*. Left to right, back row: Martha Ansfield-Scrase, Phoebe Haines, Emily Thomas. Front row: Rupert Baldwin, Mac Bexon, Roland Singer-Kingsmith.

Kingsford Community School, 2007. The College has formed a partnership with HSBC and Kingsford Community School in London's East End. Two pupils will be selected from Kingsford each year to board at Brighton College for their Sixth Form years. KCS does not have a Sixth Form, fourteen per cent of pupils are refugees and over fifty languages are spoken in the playground. Funding from HSBC will enable some talented London children to benefit from sharing in the world of Brighton College and in their turn to enrich our community. Joan Deslandes, their Head Teacher, is seen with the Headmaster and some of her pupils.

Richard Cairns, Headmaster (2006-). Since he took up his appointment he has shown himself to be a man of vision. His approach may be less frenetic than his predecessor's but our two twenty-first century Headmasters share the determination to provide a broad-based education which will nurture their pupils, mind, body and soul, and inspire them to reach for the stars. Richard Cairns has already put forward initiatives which have made the head-lines but they are based on sound educational factors which look to the future. The extraordinary growth in the influence of China makes the introduction of Mandarin to the curriculum a logical step. In keeping with the beliefs of our founding fathers, the Headmaster has a strong personal faith, but he also knows that our world is far-removed from mid-Victorian England. He seeks to ensure that his pupils are well prepared to face the challenges of this century.

Other local titles published by Tempus

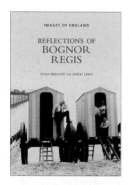

Bognor Regis

SYLVIA ENDACOTT AND SHIRLEY LEWIS

Bognor Regis today is a vibrant seaside resort. As well as boasting one of the oldest piers in Britain the town is known for Billy Butlin and his impact on bringing bucket-loads of holiday makers to the resort. Visitors and residents old and new will enjoy seeing the faces of the people and the buildings over the centuries that have made Bognor Regis what it is today.

978 07524 4299 0

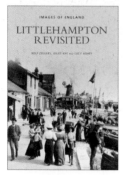

Littlehampton Revisited

ROLF ZEEGERS, JULIET NYE AND LUCY ASHBY

Littlehampton is located along the south coast next to the river Arun, and has always been a popular venue with holiday makers. This exciting and fascinating selection of over 200 old photographs covers every aspect of social life in the town. Littlehampton Museum staff have put together this fascinating insight into life in the town through the eye of a camera lens, and it stands as a testament to the communities past and present.

978 0 7524 3987 7

Haunted Guildford

PHILIP HUTCHINSON

Haunted Guildford contains a chilling range of ghostly accounts. From tales of a piano-playing spirit at Guildford Museum and a spectral monk who wanders up Friary Street, to stories of a poltergeist at the Three Pigeons public house and sightings of a ghostly woman on Whitmoor Common, this selection is sure to appeal to anyone interested in the supernatural history of the area.

978 0 7524 3826 9

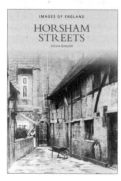

Horsham Streets

SYLVIA BARLOW

A thriving and bustling market town, Horsham is a place with a sense of its own identity. From its early origins it is well known for its sheep, cattle and corn markets with charters for the markets having been granted by the King from the thirteenth century. Many streets are covered, from the first streets named simply North, South, East and West to Belloc Close and Shelley Court after the famous poets who once lived around Horsham. This absorbing book captures Horsham's heritage and offers a unique glimpse into the town's past.

978 07524 4305 8

If you are interested in purchasing other books published by Tempus, or in case you have difficulty finding any Tempus books in your local bookshop, you can also place orders directly through our website

www.tempus-publishing.com